# Soccer Strategies

## defensive and attacking tactics

*by Robyn Jones with Tom Tranter*

# Library of Congress Cataloging - in - Publication Data

Jones, Robyn
**SOCCER STRATEGIES • Defensive and Attacking Tactics**

ISBN No. 1-890946-32-X
Library of Congress Catalog Card Number 99-74796
Copyright © September 1999

*Art Direction, Layout*
Kimberly N. Bender

*Editing and Proofing*
Bryan R. Beaver

*Printed by*
DATA REPRODUCTIONS
Auburn Hills, Michigan

**REEDSWAIN BOOKS AND VIDEOS**
612 Pughtown Road
Spring City, Pennsylvania 19475 USA
1-800-331-5191 • www.reedswain.com

**To Dad, for taking me to Goodison
and to Mam, for letting him!**

# CONTENTS

# INTRODUCTION

**W**ithin the broad world of competitive sports, there have been a number of attempts to classify activities based on certain criteria. For example, the term 'invasion games' has been used to define and group those activities, one of which is Soccer, where a crucial element is to invade or encroach the opponents' territory; the ultimate aim being to score more goals or points. Identifying the essence of the game of soccer as such assists in understanding the concepts of opposites within it, and draws attention to the idea of counter-attacking play in relation to both attacking and defending.

Taken at face value, to consider defending as part of attacking play and vice versa may appear to be a contradiction, or at the very least confusing. On further analysis however, it becomes obvious that when, where and how a team wins or loses possession of the ball is crucial in terms of implementing effective opposite strategies. It should therefore be understood that attacking and defending must be appreciated as part of the same process, even though they can be viewed as opposites. Within this context, two sets of principles emerge, one where a team has possession of the ball (attacking) and, secondly, when not in possession (defending). The former is predicated on the creation and exploitation of open areas, leading to penetration of the opponents' defense and, ultimately, to goal scoring opportunities. More specifically, such offensive principles include support, width, penetration, mobility and improvisation. Conversely, defending is primarily concerned with denying space and time to opponents in possession, thus preventing the creation of goal scoring opportunities. Appropriate principles in this context include depth, delay, concentration, team balance, cover and restraint. Experienced players and coaches understand the critical significance of moments when possession changes hands, resulting in a corresponding switch of principles.

Although successful offensive and defensive play is based on knowledge and implementation of the basic principles alluded to, we assume that such principles are already familiar to the reader. Consequently, the purpose of this book is to build on such firm foundations and to further provide an insight into the intricacies of various team formations from both attacking and defensive viewpoints. Thus, this book is primarily aimed at the intermediate or advanced coach, with the objective of raising awareness and increasing understanding of the various tactics and strategies commonly used in the modern game, and how such formations can be effectively opposed and countered.

By specifically focusing on certain aspects and not others within the text, a selective or interpretative approach is employed, which inevitably reflects personal bias' as to what is considered important. Indeed, perhaps the unique feature of this book is that it adopts such an approach to soccer formations rather than being purely descriptive. Although it can be said with relative certainty that many coaches will not agree wholly with every aspect of the text, the interpretative approach, it is hoped, will give rise to further ideas, discussion and ultimately progression in tactical soccer thinking. The goal however, is not to present the 'best way to play', as we believe that any system can be effective if both attack and defense are balanced and well executed. This is deemed particularly so when players are clear in their respective roles and responsibilities, both as individuals and as members of a larger unit. Rather, the objective of this book, in addition to providing a comprehensive description of the principle formations currently involved in modern soccer is to encourage the reader to undertake some self-evaluation of personal tactical beliefs and preferences through the promotion of a flexible analysis to coaching. It therefore proceeds under the assumption that thought and inquiry from players and coaches alike must be encouraged and accommodated if stagnation and complacency within strategic soccer thinking are to be avoided. Consequently, through providing the necessary insights for developing the ability to recognize opposition patterns of play and to correspondingly execute counteractive tactics, the text aims to encourage individuality, initiative and confidence within coaches to implement pro-active and re-active strategies as appropriate.

In relation to the structure of the book, it was decided to cite defensive formations first, as the defensive unit is often considered the foundation of the team, where clear organization is of paramount importance. Echoing the old coaching adage that one 'must build from the back', it was decided to follow this format, with a clearer picture of the overall differing formations likely to emerge once such foundations had been set. Incorporated within the analysis of principal modern defensive formations, in addition to definitions and description, are evaluation and discussion, not only of their recognized strengths and weaknesses, but also of certain key points which are considered crucial to their respective effective workings. Finally, defensive issues in relation to anticipated major questions facing coaches are outlined and addressed. The second half of the book is devoted to attacking systems, adopting a similar format of description punctuated by interpretation and evaluation. Likewise, a section on major offensive issues is also included.

Each chapter begins with a summary of its content, enabling information to be easily located. Such a structure allows the reader to dip into the book as desired, although it is acknowledged that certain later sections are grounded in earlier discussions, as attacking and defensive formations are viewed as complimentary aspects of the same process. Being very aware that graphics can often express concepts far more clearly than words, particularly in such a visually dominated arena as sport, we have attempted to incorporate many diagrams in the text to aid understanding. Within this context, and to further ease interpretation through standardized presentation, all defenders in the book are depicted as black circles ● while attackers are represented by white squares □.

Although the book is primarily aimed at intermediate and advanced coaches, we believe that others involved in soccer (e.g. players, referees and administrators) would also find it interesting, as it provides much thought provoking material for those who seek a greater understanding of the game. Finally, whereas most sports coaching books concentrate on technical skills and/or practices to be employed in the training process, we believe that the future will demand a more sophisticated approach to team play and tactical awareness. This book aims to provide a platform for that stage of development, which should, in the long term, contribute to the increased production of well-rounded and tactically aware coaches and players.

### Note
*Although throughout this book soccer players and coaches are referred to individually as he, this is only for the purpose of uniformity and convenience, and naturally should be read as 'he/she'.*

CHAPTER 1
# THE THREE MAN DEFENSE

## 1.1 Definition and description

## 1.2 The orthodox man-to-man marking system
The starting position of marking defenders
Advantages of the orthodox man-to-man system
Disadvantages of the orthodox man-to-man system
Calling offside in the orthodox man-to-man system

## 1.3 The zonal man-to-man marking system
Advantages of the zonal man-to-man marking system
Disadvantages of the zonal man-to-man marking system

## 1.4 The role of the sweeper
Position of the sweeper when both markers are on one side of the field
Sweeping in front of the defense

## 1.5 The zonal three man defense
The offside trap in a three man zonal defense
Advantages of the three man zonal defense
Disadvantages of the three man zonal defense

## 1.1 Definition and Description
The most common alternative to the traditional four man zonal defense is what has often been termed the man-to-man marking system. Although the three man defense is often organized along a man-to-man basis, where marking responsibilities are given to defenders to cover a corresponding number of opposing forwards leaving an additional player free, as reflective of most strategies employed within soccer, many variations of this basic pattern exist. Consequently, a more accurate term for this defensive organization would be a three man defense, in which players could just as likely be employed to patrol zones as opposed to having the strict role of marking opponents.

The three man defense operates as a unit within a wider 3-5-2 formation, that is, 3 defenders, 5 midfielders and 2 forwards. Although many variations exist on this theme, most commonly when one of the midfielders is pushed slightly forward thus giving a 3-4-1-2 shape, the foundational 3-5-2 is a common sight throughout the European game. Many teams, adopting a more cautious philosophy, adhere to a 5-3-2 formation with the hybrid wing-backs being a little more restricted in an attacking sense. Moreover, once in possession of the ball, the team shape is usually transformed into a 3-5-2 formation due to the need to offer width in attack. Undoubtedly, one of the principal attractions of the formation is that a greater number of players play in more advanced positions than the traditional 4-4-2 formation, with the wing-backs being given license to provide the aforementioned attacking width. Additionally, by deploying 5 players in the midfield, emphasis is given to dominating this area, as it is felt that herein lies the key to success. Diagram 1.1 illustrates the basic shape of the 3-5-2 formation incorporating a three man defense.

**Diagram 1.1** *The 3-5-2 formation.*

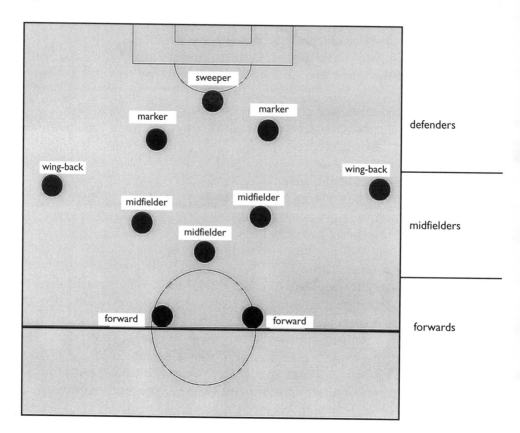

As stated earlier, there are many ways in which a three man defense can be organized. The principal strategic variations within the general framework are the zonal system, the zonal man-to-man with sweeper defense, and the orthodox man-to-man with sweeper defense. The subtleties inherent in all three variations of the system dictate the role and responsibilities of each of the three defenders. The first 2 systems to be discussed here, namely the orthodox and the zonal man-to-man, have much more in common with each other than the three man zonal defense. Thus, many of the advantages, disadvantages and key issues highlighted and discussed in the first system are also applicable to the second. Similarly, the three man zonal defense system is organized and operated along similar lines and principles to the four man zonal defense discussed in the next chapter, and thus, is confronted and surrounded by similar issues, although not exclusively so.

## 1.2 The Orthodox Man-to-Man Marking System

Reflecting its name, this defensive strategy usually employs two central marking players to cover two central opposing forwards. Each defender is allocated a particular forward to cover or mark all game, wherever the player goes. Taken to the extreme, the marker may even end up in the opposition dressing room at half time and full time! The message given is clear, in that the marker's job is to stop his forward from scoring; that is his contribution to the team and little else is expected from him. The third player, often termed the 'sweeper' or 'libero' is, as the latter name suggests, the free player within the system. He is generally not allocated any marking responsibilities, and is principally employed in a covering capacity behind the marking players. As opposed to the markers, the sweeper's role need not be totally defensive however, as the position allows great freedom, as will be demonstrated in the ensuing discussion a little later in the chapter. Suffice to say that in the basic or orthodox man-to-man defense, the sweeper's primary function is to cover the markers, giving often needed depth to the defense.

In addition to possessing the basic defensive attributes of good anticipation and patience, a principal quality required by the markers to ensure that the orthodox marking system functions effectively is a high level of physical conditioning. The task of following or 'tracking', to use a common soccer term, a single player for 90 minutes can be physically arduous, sometimes extremely so. Thus, marking players must be prepared and able to handle such a physical workload, primarily in terms of their running power.

Due to the lack of cover that the system offers in comparison to the four man zonal defense, it is imperative that the markers stay between their allocated forwards and the goal, stay on their feet as much as possible, and avoid allowing the forwards time and space to turn with the ball and run at the defense. As the wing-backs generally play in more advanced positions than the traditional full-backs, this leaves large areas on the wings into which opposing forwards can run to receive the ball. Thus, under the orthodox man-to-man system with the defender needing to 'track' his allotted forward on every run made, conditioning becomes a crucial issue.

Although inevitably tackling and physical contact are necessary parts of their game, orthodox markers are expected to stay on their feet and get involved in much less confrontational tackles than a traditional center-half or 'stopper'. There are primarily two reasons for this. Firstly, if a marker commits himself to an interception or a tackle and is beaten, more often than not, the defense is then exposed in a 2 versus 2 situation, with the attacker in possession bearing down with momentum on the sweeper, who in turn can expect little or no cover. The second factor responsible for the lesser significance of tackling in the marker's role relates to the basic or traditional starting position often adopted by defenders.

As defenders are traditionally taught to mark their opponents over the 'inside' shoulder, opportunities to regain possession are limited if passes are played into the vacated 'outside' channels (see Diagram 1.2). Consequently, the markers are often unable to tackle or intercept in such a situation.

### Diagram 1.2
*Defenders are traditionally taught to mark or cover the inside shoulder of the opponent. If this occurs in a three man defense, large areas (shaded) are left uncovered into which forwards can run to receive the ball.*

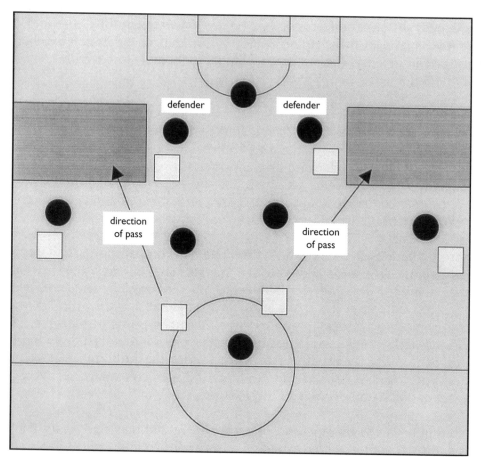

In many circumstances, and particularly within the traditional zonal back four, this defensive starting position makes good sense, as forwards need to be driven away from the central area, particularly if no additional central cover exists. However, when utilizing a system incorporating 2 markers and a sweeper, such logic does not necessarily apply.

### The starting position of marking defenders

By adopting the traditional inside line marking position, the pass to the outside channel, as illustrated in Diagram 1.2, is conceded. Thus, as previously stated, little opportunity for a defensive interception is possible, while the opposition has been allowed to gain possession deep in the defending team's territory. However, if a marking position is adopted which alternatively covers the outside shoulder of the forward, such a penetrating pass can, to a certain degree, be prohibited. The danger in adopting such an apparently aggressive marking position comes from the pass straight down the middle, which could catch the marker on the 'wrong' side of the forward, thus isolating the sweeper in a 1 versus 1 situation. Moreover, this need not be the case if the markers, by adopting an outside shoulder marking position, do so in a sideways or half turned stance. Consequently, if the ball is played down the middle, they would be able to adjust their positions quickly, and stay between the forwards and the goal. Additionally, their starting positions would threaten the pass to the outside channels, as seen in Diagram 1.3.

The pass through the middle could be further inhibited by deploying a midfielder in a deeper, more central position, thus effectively acting as a sweeper in front of the defense. Through such adjustments, the central defensive area is reinforced, while any pass now played into the outside channel shaded area could be liable to defensive interception (see Diagram 1.3). Furthermore, the defender's sideways stance should enable him to quickly adjust and adopt a more traditional defensive position if, and when, the forward receives possession. The key to the successful execution of such a strategy relies on the anticipation of the pass and reactive speed of the defenders. Additionally, any longer passes over the top of the defense should be covered by the sweeper through providing depth (see Diagram 1.3).

### Advantages of the orthodox man-to-man marking system

The basic strength of the orthodox man-to-man marking system is its clear allocation of defensive responsibilities. Each marker is allotted a forward to cover throughout the game, wherever the latter may go. The marker is not restricted by real or imagined territorial boundaries as often haunt the zonal defender, and is thus clearer in the understanding of his task obligations. In this respect, the burden of decision making has, to a certain degree, been lifted from him. His job, first and foremost, is to stop his man from scoring; if this is accomplished, then he can generally be satisfied with his game.

A further perceived strength of the system is that it enables a greater number of players to generally play in more advanced areas of the field. Thus, by not adhering to a four man defense, the central fulcrum of the team is moved to the midfield; an area often considered crucial if a favorable outcome is to be achieved. A final discernible advantage of the system is the natural defensive depth offered by the sweeper.

**Diagram 1.3**
*Defenders marking on the 'outside' shoulder thus inhibiting the pass into the 'outside' channel (shaded area). Passes into this area now are much more liable to interception.*

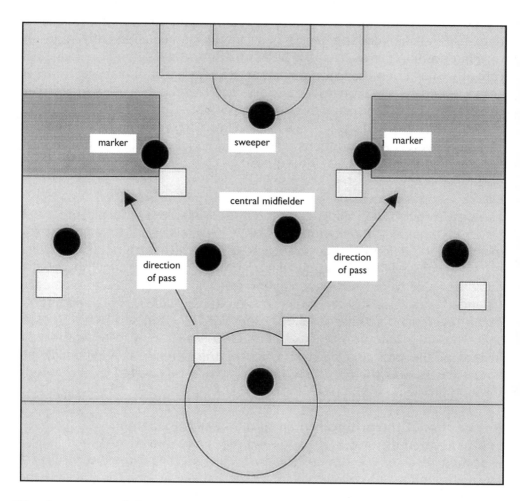

### Disadvantages of the orthodox man-to-man system
The principal weakness of the orthodox man-to-man marking system is the lack of defensive cover it offers, particularly in comparison to the four man zonal defense. If a marker is beaten, or one of the defenders is caught out of

position, the defense is immediately vulnerable as its numerical advantage has been lost. A similar problem could also occur if the midfielders fail to pick up their opposing counterparts as the latter attempt to get forward in support of an attack. Again in such a scenario the numerical advantage is lost.

A criticism often aimed at the man-to-man marking system involves the covering role of the sweeper behind the markers, and the resulting temptation for the defense to sit too 'deep', that is, too close to its own goal. If this occurs, it causes the defensive unit to become divorced from the rest of the team, and leaves the midfield players to cover larger areas than is practical to do so effectively. Such a situation invites penetrating forward passes by the opposition into the space in front of the defense.

However, although one of the principal roles of the sweeper is to supply natural depth to the defense, particularly to cover the longer pass over it, a defensive unit organized in this way should not necessarily have to defend deep. As will be discussed in the following section, an offside trap can be employed by the sweeper if a forward is pushed up onto him, thus enabling the defense to move up closer to the midfield, thereby solidifying overall team defense. Such a strategy however, should be well rehearsed, with the responsibilities of each defender within the system being clearly understood. Thus, the dangers of the defensive unit lying too deep in relation to the rest of the team need not be any more of an issue in the man-to-man system than in any other defensive formation.

A final criticism aimed at the orthodox man-to-man defensive system involves the debate surrounding the position of the sweeper when both markers have been pulled over to one side of the field. The issue surrounds the question of whether the sweeper should cover the markers, or the space on the other side of the field. The perceived weakness of the system centers on the uncertainty that if the sweeper covers the markers, the other wing is exposed to opposing midfielders running on to cross-field passes, while if he alternatively safeguards this space, the markers are left with inadequate cover. This dilemma and a suggested solution are examined in depth later under the heading 'The role of the sweeper'.

### Calling offside in the orthodox man-to-man system

The perception that the orthodox man-to-man system offers little opportunity to catch straying opposing forwards offside is not strictly true. If operated properly, an offside trap can be just as effectively used by an orthodox man-to-man defensive unit as any other. Naturally, the key lies in the allocation of roles and responsibilities and strict adherence to them.

Within the orthodox man-to-man defensive unit, all offside calls and decisions should be made by the sweeper, who is almost always the last defender. Consequently, the other defenders and midfielders should be under strict instructions not to drift, or allow themselves to be pulled by their opponents, behind the sweeper. If opponents, as they are prone to do against an ortho- dox sweeper, try to force him into marking an opponent by pushing a forward up against him, his principal response could be the springing of the offside trap (see Diagram 1.4).

Diagram 1.4 illustrates the sweeper's movement in 'stepping up' in front of the forward who has been pushed up onto him just before the ball is played through, thus stranding the forward offside. The sweeper is able to do this through good anticipation of the forward pass, while also possessing confid- ence in the knowledge that none of his teammates have drifted behind him.

**Diagram 1.4**
*The sweeper 'steps up' (S1 to S2) to catch the forward who has been pushed up against him in an offside position just before the ball is played.*

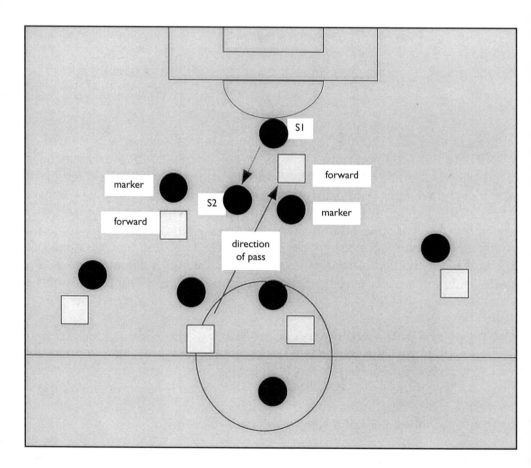

The role of the forward's original marker here is usually to cover the space in front of the defense to inhibit any passes to the forwards' feet.

### 1.3  The zonal man-to-man marking system
Many of the general advantages, disadvantages and key issues of the orthodox man-to-man system are also true for the zonal man-to-man. The characteristics discussed here therefore reflect those that differentiate it from the earlier discussed system, both negatively and positively.

The zonal man-to-man defensive system operates on very similar principles to the orthodox man-to-man, with marking defenders taking a forward each, and a sweeper, who has no marking responsibilities, giving depth to the defense. The difference lies in the fact that the defenders don't follow their players everywhere as in the orthodox man-to-man system, but rather operate as right and left sided markers. Thus, if the forwards cross to opposite sides of the field, rather than following them unquestioningly, the markers simply swap forwards (see Diagram 1.5).

### Diagram 1.5
*As the forwards cross over, the markers remain right and left sided defenders, swapping forwards as the latter enter their respective zones. The outside line marking position is easily and readily adopted.*

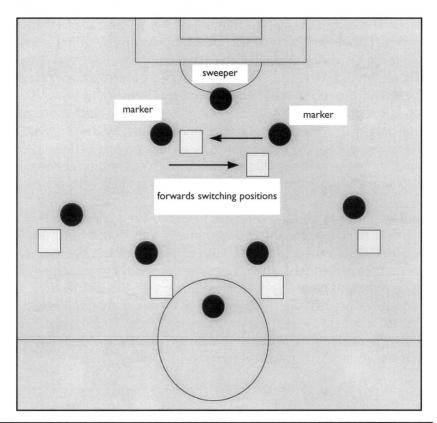

Although the system is usually termed the zonal man-to-man defense, it would be incorrect to assume that each defender is limited to a single side of the field. Consequently, if both attackers are drawn to one wing, they will still be shadowed by both defenders. The defenders however, as a general rule, will not cross, therefore remaining on definite sides of a defensive unit.

### Advantages of the zonal man-to-man marking system

When compared with the orthodox man-to-man system, the zonal man-to-man has some perceived advantages. Principal among these is that the markers' physical conditioning doesn't necessarily have to match that of the forwards. Thus, the defender can afford to wait for a forward to run into his area of responsibility, picking him up half way into, or at the end of, his run. Usually, as a consequence, a little less ground needs to be covered by the defender in this system than in the orthodox man-to-man system, which as the game wears on, enables the markers to maintain a high degree of strength and sharpness. Related to this point, by deploying right and left defensive markers, a wider area can more naturally be covered than when using the orthodox man-to-man system.

When using the zonal man-to-man system, by picking up the forwards as they enter the respective defensive zones of responsibility, the outside shoulder marking position is easily and readily obtained by the defensive marking players. While in the orthodox man-to-man defensive system, markers must work very hard to consistently achieve this position, within the zonal man-to-man unit, this is much more naturally achieved with considerably less physical effort. The defenders, in effect, are already in position to adopt such a stance when the forwards enter their vicinity. Diagram 1.5 clearly illustrates this point. Again, to successfully execute such an aggressive defending strategy, sharpness, anticipation and a sideways posture are required by the markers. As with the earlier discussed orthodox man-to-man system, if an offside trap is employed it would work on similar principles, with the responsibility for its efficient execution resting with the sweeper.

### Disadvantages of the zonal man-to-man defensive system

One of the perceived disadvantages of the system is that it becomes vulnerable when decisions must be made in relation to swapping forwards. This becomes particularly evident when the latter are constantly changing positions from left to right and back again. During such times, the lack of clear role allocation about whom to mark when and where can become problematic, although to a much lesser extent than in pure zonal defensive units. Nevertheless, as with all zonal marking defenses, it is during such times of transition that the system is considered to be at its weakest.

### 1.4 The role of the sweeper

The role of the sweeper in both the orthodox and zonal man-to-man marking systems is very similar. His primary function is to operate as a spare player, the final covering defender who generally has no marking responsibilities. Being the final outfield player in the team's formation, and thus having the play almost exclusively in front of him, he is in an excellent position to view the game. Consequently, he is often expected to take responsibility not only for organizing the defensive unit, but also for adjusting the team's formation should this be deemed necessary. In many ways he is the coach on the field, particularly in a defensive sense.

As already discussed, he should be responsible for operating the offside strategy when, and if, appropriate. Similarly, he is almost exclusively responsible for covering, not only the markers, but also the space behind the defense (see Diagram 1.6). Thus, much lateral movement is involved in his game.

### Diagram 1.6
*The sweeper is responsible for covering not only the markers, but also longer passes played into the shaded area behind the defense.*

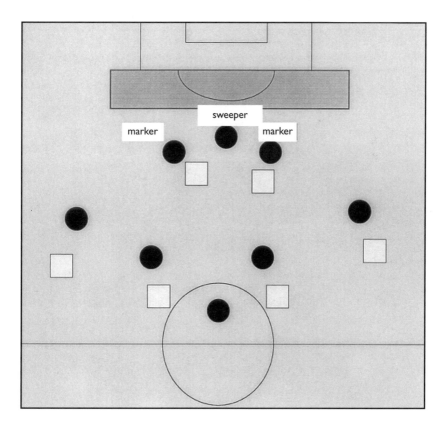

Although generally he is free from marking responsibilities, certain occasions do arise when he must be drawn into the play to fulfill such a function. A primary example of such a situation is when a marker has 'lost' his forward. The sweeper should assume responsibility to mark the open forward until the original marker has recovered his position. Naturally, it is during such time that the defense is vulnerable as it has lost its numerical superiority. When such a situation occurs, resulting in no defensive cover being available, the starting position of the marking defenders requires adjustment. A more traditional inside shoulder marking position should now be assumed. By adopting such a stance, defenders ensure that they are in a position to cover incisive passes into the space behind the defense. Conversely however, the space in front of the defense is largely uncovered; thus, less penetrating passes to the feet of the forwards are conceded (see Diagram 1.7). Once the recovering marker is back in position, the sweeper becomes the free man, and the defensive unit is again intact.

**Diagram 1.7**
*If the sweeper is forced into becoming a marker, the natural defensive cover offered by the system is lost. An inside line marking position should now be adopted by the sweeper and marker, while awaiting the beaten defender to recover his position.*

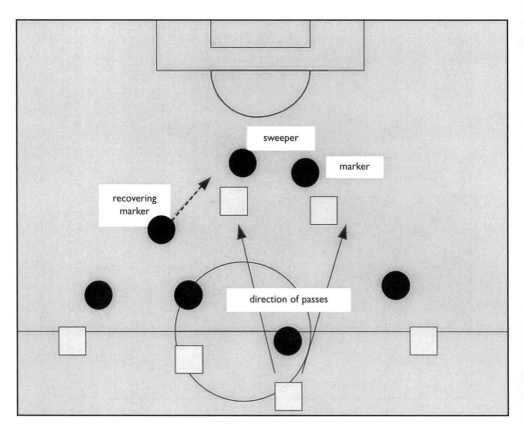

Another situation when the sweeper must actively engage himself in a ball winning or confrontational encounter with a member of the opposition occurs when the latter, usually a midfield player, is running at the defense with or without the ball. If the opposing midfielder is in possession, it is the sweeper who must forsake his covering role to step up and meet the threat. This enables the markers to keep concentrating on their principal job of covering their allocated forwards, and maintains clear role responsibility among members of the defensive unit. If the opposing midfielder is running towards the defense without the ball, as a rule, the sweeper should pick him up as he ventures in advance of the forwards, thus not conceding his covering position until absolutely necessary. He is now in a position to step up in front of the on-running midfielder to catch him offside. As emphasized earlier, care must be taken to ensure that this is timed to perfection to catch the stranded opponent in an offside position as the ball is played.

### Diagram 1.8
*If the sweeper concentrates only on covering the marking players, who have been drawn to one wing, large areas on the opposite side of the field are vulnerable to runs from upcoming midfield players.*

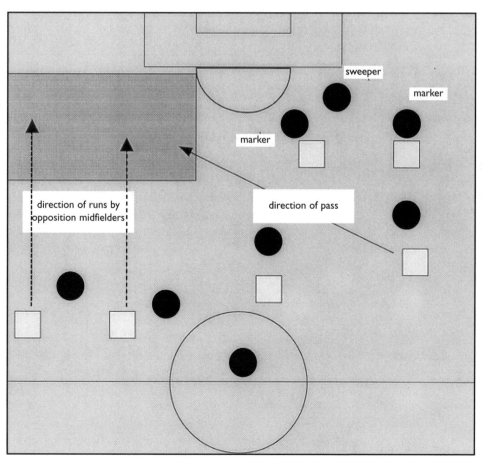

**Position of sweeper when both markers are on one side of the field**

An issue previously touched upon, which will now be explored in depth, is the apparent dilemma facing the sweeper concerning his position when both markers have been pulled over by the forwards to one side of the field. To cover the markers in this respect as in Diagram 1.8 would leave a large area on the opposite wing unguarded, and thus vulnerable to opposition midfielders running from deep positions.

Remembering that his responsibility is to cover space as well as players, the sweeper's position in this instance should be slightly removed from the markers; close enough to give them a degree of cover, but also so that he can guard the vulnerable area on the opposite side of the defense, as illustrated in Diagram 1.9. In this way, if an opposition midfield player were to break away into the space created, the sweeper would be able to cover his run.

**Diagram 1.9**

*By adjusting his position in such a way, the sweeper is able to cover both the markers and the cross field pass to the opposite wing. To accommodate such a strategy, the position of each marker is slightly adjusted to adopt more of an inside line marking stance.*

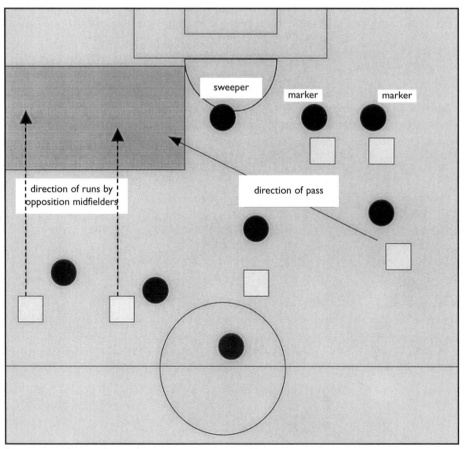

If the sweeper adopts such a strategy, there are implications for the marking positions of his 2 defensive teammates. As the natural covering position of the sweeper has been, to a certain extent, compromised, they must now adopt an inside marking line, first and foremost protecting the space behind the defense (see Diagram 1.9).

### Sweeping in front of the defense

Although in the vast majority of cases, the sweeper is deployed as a covering player behind the markers, this need not be exclusively so. As he is not restricted by marking responsibilities, he consequently has the freedom to bring the ball up-field to often initiate attacks. He is able to do this because it is unlikely that any of the opposing midfielders have been designated the responsibility to challenge him should he venture forward, particularly if they are involved in their own individual midfield contests.

Furthermore, having ventured forward, the sweeper may remain in a deep midfield position for a significant part of the game, effectively sweeping in front of the defense. Such a decision may be taken in order to bolster the midfield, who could appear to be losing the battle for control in that particular area. Alternatively, the move may be prompted by the need to prevent and/or to intercept passes to the feet of the opposing forwards, which could be an instrumental tactic in the opposition's game plan. Inevitably, if such a role is undertaken by the sweeper, the more conservative inside line marking position should be adopted by the other defenders to protect the critical space behind the defense, as the sweeper is no longer employed in his more traditional covering role (see Diagram 1.10).

## 1.5 The zonal three man defense

The zonal three man defense operates along similar principles to the four man zonal defense examined in the next chapter, and consequently it shares many of the latter's strengths and weaknesses. Unlike the orthodox and zonal man-to-man variations, within the three man zonal defensive unit no member is exempt from marking responsibilities, and all are engaged in such duties as opponents enter their respective zones. The players comprising the unit generally do not cross, and therefore operate as right, center and left zone defenders. If a forward is involved in a lateral run across the defense, he is simply passed on to the defender whose zone he enters.

### The offside trap in a three man zonal defense

Within a zonal defense, such a strategy can be implemented in one of two ways. Firstly, responsibility for calling offside can be given to the 2 flank or wing defenders as they are in a position to look laterally across the defensive line. Thus, if the defense is attacked on its right wing, the left wing defender should give the call to either hold the defensive line or to step up-field in an

## Diagram 1.10

*If a sweeper operates in front of the defense, the markers must adjust their positions and adopt a more conservative inside line marking stance.*

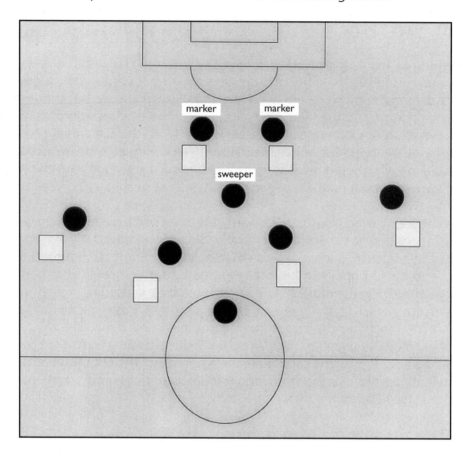

attempt to catch an opposing player offside. He is able to make such a call with confidence as he should be the last defender; the wing backs (and the other midfielders) having been given strict instructions not to drift behind him (see Diagram 1.11). Such a principle is sometimes similarly employed in the four man zonal defense, where the full backs are given such a responsibility: a strategy discussed in depth a little later.

When operated in this way it is often possible to draw a straight line along the defensive unit, indicating its swivel properties, the hub of which is the middle defender. Thus, if it is being attacked down one wing, the defensive unit is organized in such a way that it represents a diagonal line with the wing defender nearest to the ball being covered by the central defender, who in turn is covered by the other wing defender (see Diagram 1.11).

The main criticism of organizing a defensive strategy in this way centers on the distance between the 2 wing defenders and their ability to execute such a crit-

## Diagram 1.11

*The forward has been allowed to run into an offside position by the wing defend-er who is in a position to see across the defensive unit. The defensive unit, in turn, is organized along a straight line.*

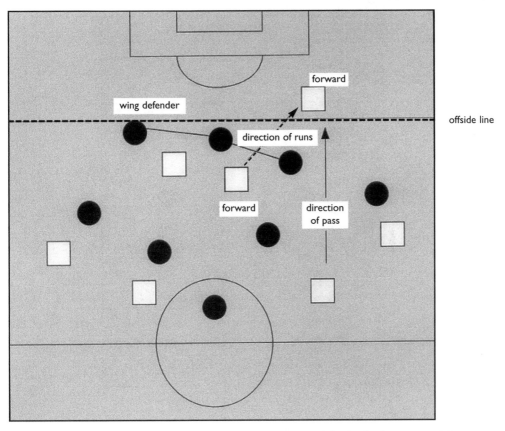

ical maneuver from a peripheral position. Thus, although they are able to see clearly along the defensive line, their sometimes marginal positions make it difficult to correctly judge the offside call, particularly if they are far apart and/or if numerous forward runs by different attackers are being made.

The second means by which an offside trap could be organized in a three man zonal defense is by giving responsibility for such an action to the middle defender in the unit. Thus, the instruction to step up or to hold the defensive line in the hope of catching opposition attackers offside would be solely his responsibility. As opposed to being organized on a swivel principle, with a straight line linking all three members of the defensive unit (Diagram 1.11), a defense organized in this way would be structured along the pattern of an inverted 'V' (see Diagram 1.12).

The principal advantage of organizing the offside trap in such a way rests on the proximity of the central defender to the decisive action much of the time.

### Diagram 1.12
*The forward has been allowed to run into an offside position by the central member of the defensive unit. The unit is organized along the lines of inverted 'V'.*

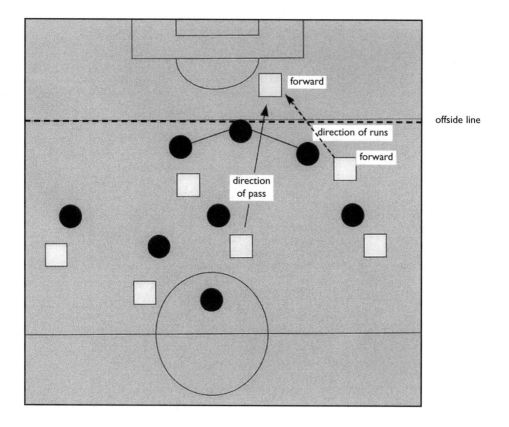

Additionally, on a more practical level, the player occupying such a role is usually one of the most dominant and experienced in the team and is generally very well able to judge and execute such a tricky ploy. The principal key to success here is that the other players must adhere to strict instructions not to go behind the central defender in any circumstance without his knowledge.

By adopting an inverted 'V' shape, the central defender in the unit, although still operating in a middle defensive zone, adopts many of the characteristics of the sweeper in the two previously mentioned systems. Similarly, by being the last outfield player, if the opposition tries to force him into a more active marking role by pushing a forward onto him, he has the option of stepping up when appropriate to catch the forward offside. He is able to take such action being theoretically secure in the knowledge that he is indeed the last outfield defender.

## Advantages of the three man zonal defense

The main advantage of organizing a three man defensive unit along zonal lines relates to the greater width of area naturally covered by such a unit when compared to the earlier discussed man-to-man systems. Forwards are passed on as they enter the different zones. The shape of the defensive unit is, therefore, more constant and easier to maintain, which allows both forwards and spaces to be covered simultaneously. A further perceived strength of the system is the ability to 'hold' the defensive line, making it easier to catch opposing forwards offside. However, as has been demonstrated, an offside trap can be implemented successfully by any defensive system if it is well rehearsed and players are aware of their responsibilities within it.

## Disadvantages of the three man zonal defense

The disadvantages of the three man zonal defense system mainly center on the lack of clear allocation of marking responsibilities in relation to each member of the defensive unit. As with any zonal formation, when forwards are in the process of being passed on, or between defenders, the system is at its most vulnerable. Uncertainty about who should mark a forward as he leaves one zone and enters another can lead to hesitancy in the defense, resulting in a goal scoring opportunity for the attacking team. Similarly, by not allocating defenders specific forwards to mark, the defenders could be drawn into a tendency to watch the ball while their opponents find space behind and between them. Naturally, such a scenario spells great danger, with a defender being caught out of position, having 'lost' his forward.

Although one of the perceived strengths of the system, as outlined above, relates to the ability of the unit to better 'hold' a defensive line, the lack of natural depth in the unit which enables it to do precisely this is also viewed as a potential weakness. This can be partially alleviated if the unit is organized along the lines of an inverted 'V' (see Diagram 1.12), where the middle defender is charged with generally covering the other two. Nevertheless, in comparison to a unit that employs a free sweeper, the cover offered to and by defenders in a zonal system is not so clear cut.

# Chapter 2
# THE FOUR MAN DEFENSE
# THE FLAT BACK FOUR

### 2.1 Definition and description

When mention of a four man defense is made, this is commonly assumed to be organized along zonal lines, with 2 center-backs being flanked by 2 full-backs on either side. This however, need not necessarily be the case, as, on occasions, a four man defense could comprise of three central defenders and a sweeper playing behind them, although such a variation is very rare. Therefore, to keep the chapter (and indeed the whole book) within workable (and readable!) limits, this section will investigate and analyze the variations inherent in the four man zonal defensive unit. It is worth noting however, that many of the issues surrounding the three central defender and sweeper system were addressed in the previous chapter, although more specifically within the context of a three man defense.

The four man zonal defense, or the 'flat back four' to give its more common name, was, until recently, by far the most common formation used by British teams, and is generally incorporated into a 4-4-2 formation (see Diagram 2.1). Although in recent years its dominance has become increasingly challenged by other defensive systems, it remains a very widespread formation throughout the world. As mentioned earlier, the defensive unit in such an arrangement comprises of 4 players operating in pre-defined areas, including 2 center-backs and 2 full-backs (see Diagram 2.1).

The logic behind such a structure dictates that the width of the defensive area is fully covered with each player responsible for his own zone of operation. Thus, if a forward, in an attempt to find space, embarks on a lateral run across the field, each defender would assume responsibility for him as he enters his particular zone. The fine workings of such a defense can be organized in numerous ways, including the twin center-half swivel system, the four man swivel system and the sweeper-stopper system.

## 2.2 The twin center-half swivel system

The twin center-half swivel system is based on the foundational principle that each central defender complements the role of the other as the situation demands. For example, both are required to 'attack' the ball dependent on the zone the ball is delivered into, and conversely, both are expected to cover the other as necessary. They thus swivel on an axis that is positioned between

### Diagram 2.1

*The standard four man zonal defense in a standard 4-4-2 formation comprises of two central defenders, a right-back and left-back, each allocated a specific zone of responsibility.*

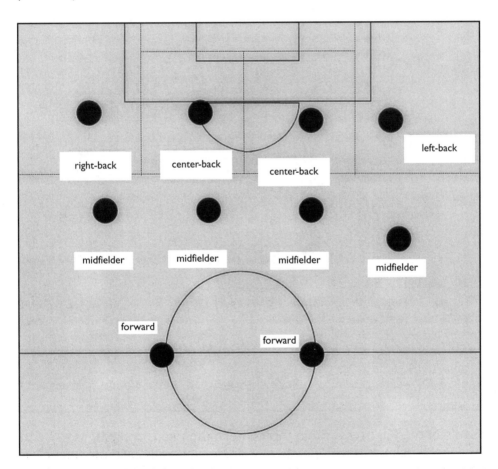

them. Within the system, their positions are usually rigidly defined by their zones of responsibility, with one considered to be a right sided central defender and the other a left.

The term 'swivel' emanates from the reaction of the second central defender once the first defender has taken the decision to 'attack' the ball. The former's responsibility in such a situation is to give depth and cover to his teammate. Alternately, when he is the first defender required to confront an opposing forward, his central defensive partner is expected to provide cover (see Diagram 2.2).

**Diagram 2.2**
*When one of the central defenders takes the initiative to 'attack' the ball, the other complements the action by dropping deeper to supply cover. Note the close proximity of both full backs to their central defensive teammates.*

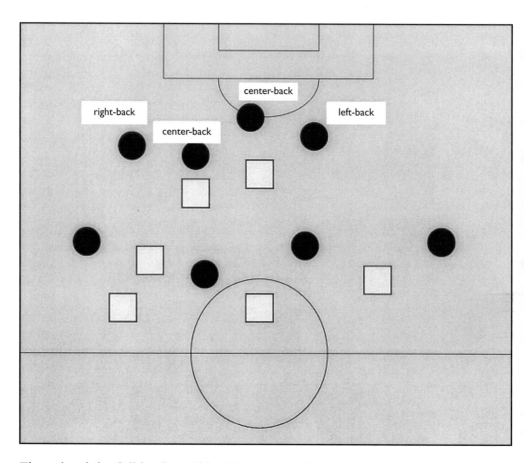

The role of the full-backs within this context also needs analysis, as to be truly effective the defense must operate as a single unit, with each member clear in his responsibilities. As many teams in the modern game favor a two central forward strike force, both central defenders within this system are often forced into marking roles for much of the time. However, if one drops deeper as a response to the other 'attacking' the ball, the former is prone to leave his forward unmarked. Consequently, the need exists for both full-backs to be in close proximity to their central defensive teammates, so that one, or either, is in a position to pick up the unmarked forward should he gain possession. By dropping a little deeper, the full-backs are additionally in position to provide extra cover should the first central defender who has gone to 'attack' the ball be beaten.

A slight variation on this theme involves both central defenders being required to tightly mark the opposing two central strikers. If such a strategy is used, the full-backs are then required to provide the cover. They are thus expected to operate a little deeper than their central defensive teammates, with the covering positions adopted being crucial to the effective workings of the system.

### 2.3  The four man swivel defense

A variation of the twin center-half swivel defense is the four man swivel defense, which is organized in such a way that enables all four defenders to mark opponents very tightly when necessary, while simultaneously being able to cover each other. Through adherence to such a system, both fellow defenders and zones are covered simultaneously, as illustrated in Diagram 2.3.

### Diagram 2.3

*If the opposition is attacking down the defense's left wing, the left-back engages the opponent in possession, with the rest of the defenders taking up positions to cover him and each other. As with the three man zonal unit, the defense is organized along a diagonal line.*

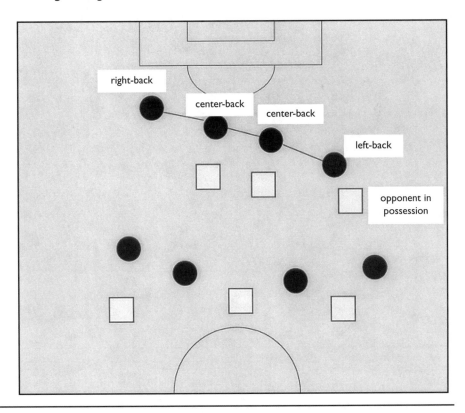

When an attack develops in a wide area, the appropriate full-back is the first defender to engage the opponent, with the nearest center-back taking up a position to cover him. The other center-back, in turn, adopts a position to cover the first center-back, while finally, completing the diagonal line, the full-back on the opposite side should cover the second center-back (see Diagram 2.3). If the team in possession switches the ball to continue the attack on the other side of the field, the defensive line is altered to follow the opposite diagonal, thereby swiveling on the central axis located between the center-backs.

## 2.4 The sweeper-stopper system

### Diagram 2.4
*One of the full-backs (here the left-back) plays in very close proximity to the center-backs in order to pick up a central striker left free as the sweeper drops back to cover. This enables the other full-back (the right-back) to move into a more advanced position to support the midfield.*

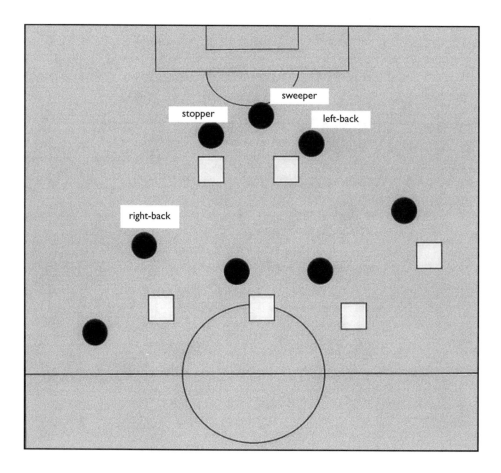

The sweeper-stopper system operates along similar lines to the twin center-half swivel structure discussed earlier. The discerning characteristic of this system however, is that one of the center-backs, the stopper, is designated to always 'attack' the ball if possible, while the other, the sweeper, drops back to provide the cover. When such a scenario occurs, one of the strikers is allowed a degree of freedom as the sweeper sacrifices his marking duties. Consequently, the full-backs must play in very close proximity to the central defenders so that one, or the other, is in a position to pick up the second striker when necessary. In order to bolster the midfield area, the full-back not engaged as such is often encouraged to push forward, enabling in turn a midfielder to venture into a more advanced position to better support the forwards (see Diagram 2.4). One of the main advantages of the system is the clear delineation of role responsibility in the center of the defense, with the sweeper always being the last man. Naturally, if the opposition play three forwards, then both full-backs will be engaged in defensive marking duties, with the sweeper's role again principally being a covering one.

## 2.5 Operating an offside trap with a four man zonal defense

The principal difference between the four man swivel system and the formation incorporating a twin center-half swivel is the covering positions adopted by the full-backs. This is particularly true of the one farthest from the ball. In the four man swivel structure he is the last defender, giving cover to the center-backs. Consequently, as he is in a position to see across the defensive line (see Diagram 2.3), he is, more often than not, given the responsibility to make the decision to 'hold' the line in an attempt to catch opposing forwards offside. Although his position allows him the best view to execute such a strategy, as mentioned in the previous discussion of the three man zonal defense, the weakness here is his possible distance from the action, particularly if the ball is on the opposite side of the field. Consequently, as he does not occupy a central position, his instructions may not be heard by the other full-back, resulting in an unworkable and dangerously flawed system.

Conversely, in the twin center-half swivel and the stopper-sweeper systems, the covering center-back or sweeper is the last defender, and should have the responsibility for calling offside. Although unlike the full-back in the four man swivel formation, he must look both ways to double check that the full-backs have not drifted into deeper areas behind him, his central location means that he is in a better position to dominate the situation and be clearly heard (see Diagram 2.2). Thus, much like the sweeper in Chapter 1, if other players are aware of the requirement not to venture behind him, he can generally organize the offside trap with clarity and confidence, and 'step up' in front of an opposing forward when appropriate, thus stranding the latter in an offside position.

The key to operating a successful offside trap utilizing a 4 (or indeed a 3) man zonal defense relies on the intensity of effort exerted by the man nearest the ball to pressure the opponent in possession. Very often, this involves a forward engaged in defensive duties. The collective advance up the field of the defensive line held by the back four defenders should be directly related to the pressure placed on the ball. Additionally, when pressure is placed on the ball carrier by the first defender, a second defender should adjust his position by covering the zone vacated by the first defender (see Diagram 2.5). Although the wing defensive players can be drawn centrally somewhat to assist in this task, the situation, in essence, calls for the second defender to cover an increased distance as a direct result of the first defender putting pressure on the ball. Thus, although a degree of width is lost as the flank players are inevitably drawn into the middle areas, central defensive solidarity throughout the team is maintained if the second defender is both physically able to execute his role in such a situation and is fully cognizant with it. If such a strategy is employed,

## Diagram 2.5
*If pressure is placed on the ball by the first defender, the defensive line is able to move up, catching opposing forwards offside. Note how the second defender nearest the ball covers the space left by the first defender who is pressuring the man in possession.*

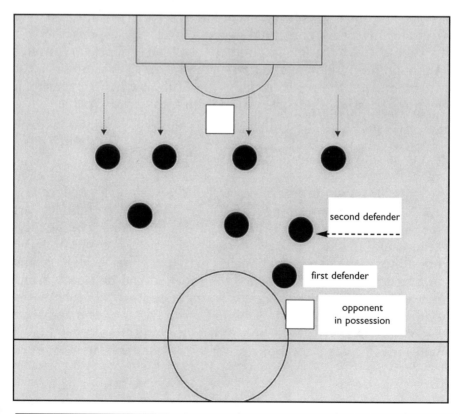

second defender

first defender

opponent
in possession

the defensive line is able to move forward, often catching opposing forwards in offside positions (see Diagram 2.5). The responsibility for calling such a maneuver is dependent on the defensive structure e.g. if the unit is organized along a twin center-half swivel, a four man swivel or a sweeper-stopper system.

The back four defenders are only able to hold such a line due to the pressure placed on the ball, which often forces the opposition to pass square or back. The tactic is grounded in the premise that the opposing player in possession is denied the time and space to play penetrating passes over and through the defense. Alternatively, if little or no pressure is placed on the ball carrier, the defense and the midfield retreat. This is done to protect the critical area behind the defense, thus denying opposition forwards the space into which to run to receive penetrating and probing passes (see Diagram 2.6). Without pressure on the ball, the opportunity to render an effective offside trap is severely lessened.

**Diagram 2.6**

*If no pressure is placed on the ball by the first defender, the defensive line drops deeper (as does the midfield) to deny the space behind it.*

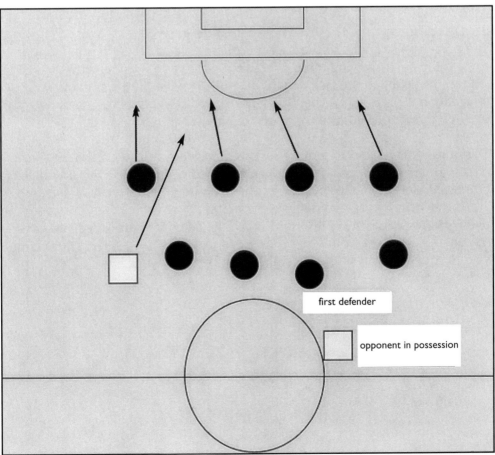

first defender

opponent in possession

## 2.6 Advantages of a four man zonal defense

The principal advantage of a four man zonal defense relates to its ability to cover both opponents and spaces across the width of the field. Consequently, it is rarely prone to defensive imbalance where defenders are dragged over by opposing forwards to one side of the field, leaving the other wing exposed to a switch of spatial focus by the attack.

Additionally, in contrast to the three man defense, having a fourth defender in the unit allows an extra degree of cover should one of the defenders be beaten. In such a scenario, provided the opposition only play with two forwards as is the modern trend, defensive numerical superiority is maintained.

The flat back four generally also has the ability to hold the defensive line to a much greater extent than a defense which employs an orthodox sweeper. Consequently, they are able to move up more effectively as a unit, not only to catch the opposition forwards offside, but also to deny opposition midfielders time and space to play penetrating passes. This is achieved through pushing their own midfield unit farther up the pitch as they advance to pressure the ball (see Diagram 2.5).

## 2.7 Disadvantages of the four man zonal defense

The perceived strength of the four man defensive zonal system in being able to hold the defensive line more effectively is seen as a weakness by some. This relates principally to the lack of natural depth inherent in the system, whichever variation is played. It is therefore sometimes susceptible to passes over and through it, e.g. played into the space behind it.

This, in turn, is related to a more serious perceived deficiency; that is, the lack of clear marking responsibilities given to the defenders. As with any defense organized along zonal principles, problems arise when forward players operate in the areas where two defensive zones meet, which can lead to confusion over role responsibility. Although as a rule defenders are adept at passing opponents on as they run from zone to zone, hesitancy resulting from confusion surrounding marking responsibility in the areas where zones meet can be a serious problem.

# Chapter 3
# DEFENSIVE ISSUES

## 3.1 Introduction

## 3.2 Stopping the 'man in the hole'
Negating the threat of the 'man in the hole' with a four man zonal defense
Negating the threat of the 'man in the hole' with a three man defense

## 3.3 How to counter a three man attack
With a four man defense
With a three man defense

## 3.4 Should defenders show 'inside' or 'outside'?
Showing the 'outside'
Showing the 'inside'

## 3.5 Organizing the defense from corner kicks
Defending corners using a zonal strategy
Defending corners using a man-to-man system

## 3.6 How to counteract pace in attack
Individual depth in defense
Collective depth on defense

## 3.1 Introduction
The aim of this chapter is to highlight some common issues faced by a defense in the attempt to combat offensive strategies and tactics. Although numerous instances could have been examined here, the five chosen represent very differing scenarios from a defensive viewpoint. These include respective discussions on negating a particular positional player, combatting a general attacking strategy, adopting a defensive ploy to slow the momentum of an attack, differing possible organizational systems at set plays and counteracting a potent offensive attribute.

## 3.2 Stopping the 'man in the hole'
Deploying a 'man in the hole' has become quite fashionable within the game during the past few years. The 'hole' in this respect refers to the space that usually exists between the traditional midfield and forward players. Although the player allocated to operate in this space could be a deeper lying forward, he is more commonly an advanced offensively minded midfielder. Thus, in the ensuing discussion, he is assumed to be the latter. Diagrams 3.1 and 3.2 illustrate his position if operating in a 3-5-2 and 4-4-2 formation utilizing two orthodox forwards, while Diagram 3.3 depicts his position in a 4-4-2 formation using one traditional forward.

### Diagram 3.1
*The 'man in the hole' (shaded area) in a 3-5-2 formation.*

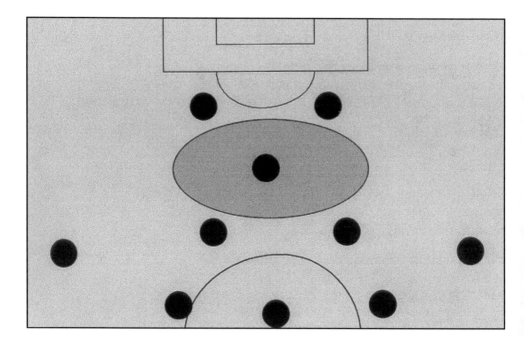

### Diagram 3.2
*The 'man in the hole' (shaded area) in 4-4-2 formation using two forwards.*

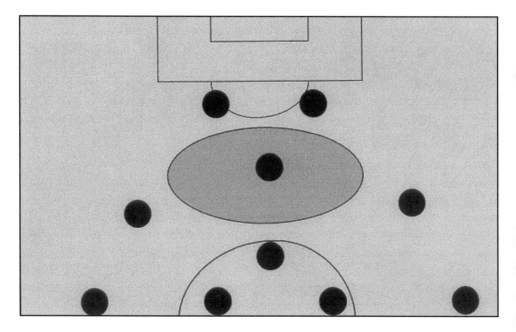

**Diagram 3.3**
*The 'man in the hole' (shaded area) in 4-4-2 formation using one forward.*

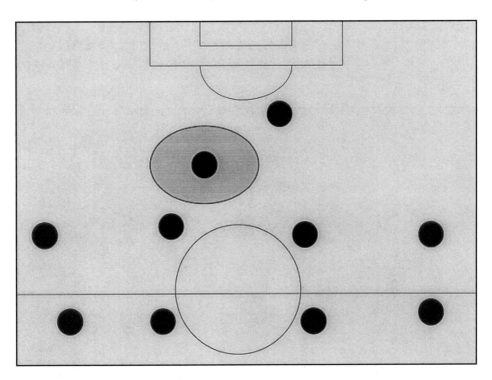

Positioning a player in such an area creates a problem for the defense in many respects. Predicaments arising from the uncertainty as to who should be responsible for the player from a defensive viewpoint are common, as he operates in a space where often no defending players are permanently stationed. Thus, defensive confusion is frequently evident related to the question of should a defender step up from the back to mark him, and, if so, which one, or should a midfielder be brought back to do the job? This decision should not be taken lightly, as very often he is a dangerous and talented attacker. However, how to best mark him and negate his threat is dependent on what sort of player he is, that is, if he is a 'passer' or a 'runner'?

Such a distinction aims to clarify if the principal danger posed by him stems from his use of the ball, or from his running off the ball. If he falls into the former category, his contribution to the attacking team emanates from his ability to engineer goal scoring opportunities for others through his passing skills. Alternatively, if he is a 'runner', his principal menace to the defense results from his constant movement both into wide areas and also in advance of the forwards, proving very elusive to mark. A more comprehensive examination of his attacking capabilities is presented a little later in Chapter 7. The defensive question still remains however, of how best to deal with this evasive opponent.

**Negating the threat of the 'man in the hole' with a four man zonal defense**

### Diagram 3.4
*The right full-back has been re-deployed to mark the advanced midfielder*
*i.e. the 'man in the hole'. The defense is now re-organized along the lines of a three*
*man defensive unit.*

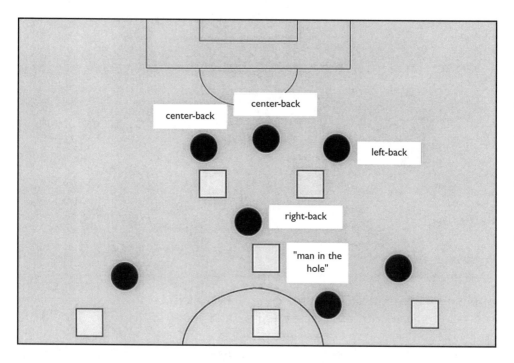

If a player operating in the 'hole' is a 'passer', then it is imperative to deny him both time and space when in possession. The obvious way to achieve this is to give either one of the four defenders or the defensive midfielder the responsibility of marking him on a man-to-man basis. If one of the defenders is given the job, more often than not it is one of the full-backs, as the center-backs are already engaged in marking two forwards. If such a strategy is adopted, the four man defensive unit is transformed into a three man zonal defense, with the full-back on the opposite side having to move closer to the 2 center-backs in order to give them a greater degree of cover. Additionally, the wing vacated by the full back designated to mark the 'man in the hole' should be covered to a significant degree by the nearest center-back through adopting the outside line marking position discussed in Chapter 1 (see Diagram 3.4).

Alternatively, if the defensive midfielder is given the task of negating the 'man in the hole', this requires one of the full-backs to push forward somewhat to reinforce the midfield area. Diagram 3.5 illustrates the team adjustment required in this regard, with again one full-back operating closer to the 2 center-backs to offer cover, while the other is pushed into a midfield supporting position as one of the original midfielders has been lost to purely defensive duties.

## Diagram 3.5
*The left-back is pushed into a greater midfield role if a central midfielder is re-deployed to defensively cover the 'man in the hole'.*

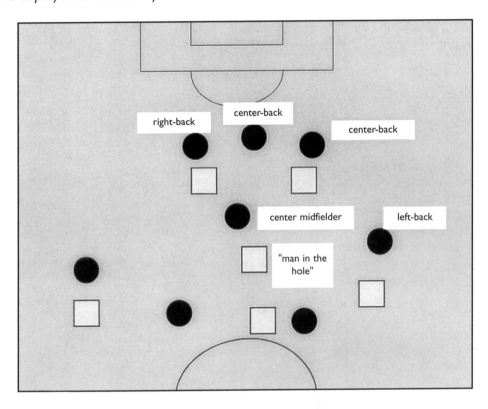

Conversely, if the attacking player operating in the advanced midfield role offers more of a threat from his running off the ball, often to positions in advance of his forwards, then he can be dealt with differently from a defensive viewpoint. In contrast to the 'passer', whose menace comes from his distributing ability and is best negated through a man marker, the 'runner' poses a different kind of problem. A marker could similarly be allotted to follow him everywhere, but certain problems sometimes emerge with this strategy. These include the fitness of the marking player, which needs to be at least the equal of the 'runner', and also the intelligence and discipline of the marker in allowing the attacker to run into offside positions when appropriate. Although he has instructions to mark his man everywhere, as a general rule, the marker is not allowed to go behind the last defender. Although such an issue is also present in the man-to-man marking defenses discussed in Chapter 1, it is a little more problematic here as the 'runner' comes from a deeper position, and the marker, having been dragged into a midfield role, is not strictly a part of the defensive unit. Correct and early decision making in such instances is vital if the defensive strategy is to stay intact, while practice and rehearsal to develop understanding and knowledge of individual role responsibility and obligation is similarly crucial.

### Diagram 3.6
*The central defensive midfield player is ideally placed to mark the 'man in the hole' when operating a 3-5-2 system.*

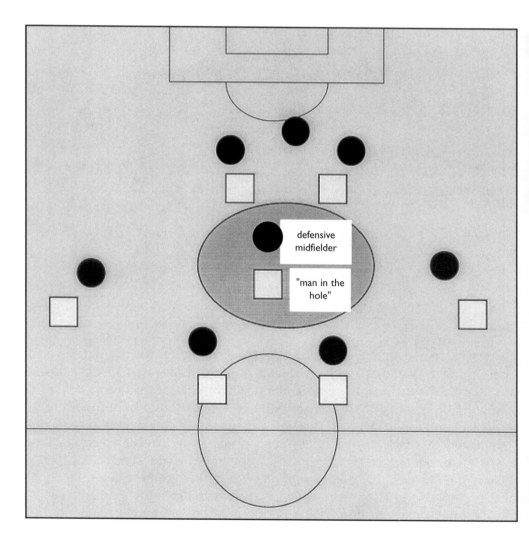

As the runner's threat comes from his ability to find spaces in the attacking third of the field, very often a preferred way to deal with his menace is to simply fill the spaces with defenders. The zonal system, in particular the four man variation, is ideally suited to execute such a strategy, with the 'runner', rather than being followed everywhere by a man marker, being picked up as he runs into the various zones of the field. He is consequently picked up by the appropriate defender either when he is well into, or at the end of his run. Moreover, if the 'man in the hole' and another forward end up occupying a single defensive zone, naturally this would necessitate the individual members of the defense to operate much closer together, allowing less room to be exploited between them, while simultaneously maintaining a numerical advantage.

### Negating the threat of the 'man in the hole' with a three man defense
If a three man defensive unit is utilized, then the issue of who should be responsible for him is much more clear cut. The natural shape of the five man midfield usually requires that one member operates in a deeper role, effectively patrolling in front of the defensive unit (see Diagram 3.6). This player is ideally placed to mark the 'man in the hole', as they largely share the same space. This would be the case if the advanced midfield player was a 'passer' or a 'runner'.

### 3.3  How to counter a three man attack
Facing a three man attack raises several issues for the defending team. Not only must the positional role of the third forward be quickly recognized, but also the nature of his game. This section aims to discuss the ways in which a defense can be organized to negate the threat from varying formations using 3 forward players, wherever and however the danger should emanate.

### How to counter a three man attack with a four man defense
Defending against a three man attack with a 'flat' back four defense in theory should not be too problematic. If the third forward is a winger or wide player, then the full-back on whichever wing the former is operating should take responsibility for marking him. If this occurs, the other full-back should adopt a closer position to the center-backs to offer cover, or be prepared to mark one of the central strikers should one drift into his zone (see Diagram 3.7).

If the third forward plays a little deeper in the 'hole', then the defensive responsibility for him could be organized in a number of ways, depending on his nature (see section 3.2). Suffice to say that a player occupying such a position often causes the defending team considerable problems if a strategy is not determined beforehand to deal with him.

## Diagram 3.7

*In a 'flat' back four defensive unit, the appropriate full-back marks the winger (i.e. the third forward), with the other full-back re-positioned closer to the center-backs in order to give greater cover.*

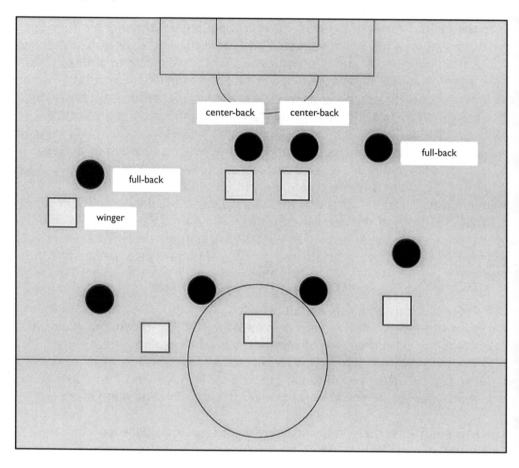

## How to counter a three man attack with a three man defense

If the third attacker is one who occupies a very advanced midfield position, the defensive responsibility for him in a three man defense is usually placed upon the defensive midfield player, as discussed earlier (see section 3.2). Thus, the deepest midfield player in a unit of five is in the ideal position to pick him up, as they tend to occupy a similar area (see Diagram 3.6). Conversely, if the third attacker is a winger, then this poses a question to the three man defense, as if no corresponding adjustment is made, its numerical superiority will be lost.

One way in which numerical superiority can be re-established is by deploying the appropriate wing-back to mark the winger. Such a ploy however, robs the defensive team of offensive width on that side when possession is won, which can lead to overall team imbalance. This becomes a crucial issue if the wing-back concerned is in the team for his attacking as opposed to his defensive, qualities, with a principal offensive weapon being lost to the team. If such a situation occurs however, one of the central midfielders tends to be re-positioned a little wider, with instructions to supply some offensive width whenever possible (see Diagram 3.8).

## Diagram 3.8

*If the wing-back is re-deployed as a full-back to mark the opposing winger, the appropriate midfielder is moved across to cover the vacated space with instructions to supply offensive width when possible.*

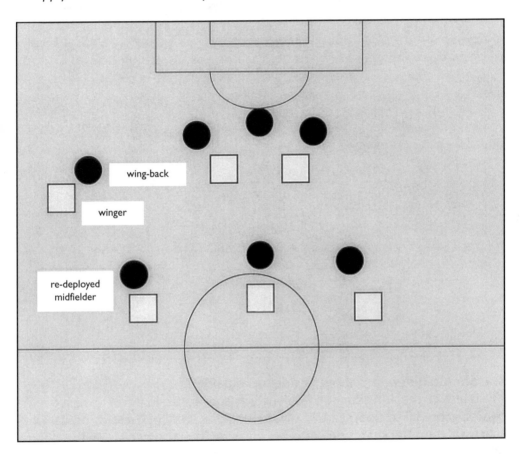

Alternatively, rather than sacrificing a potent offensive weapon to defensive duties, the appropriate wing defender from the three man defensive unit could be designated to guard the winger, while the defensive midfielder is re-positioned into a traditional back three formation. Although the numerical superiority is lost in the central midfield area, defensive solidity is maintained by having four defensively minded players occupying the back positions. At the same time, offensive width is not lost (see Diagram 3.9).

### Diagram 3.9
*If a wing defender guards the winger, the defensive central midfielder can be re-deployed into the three man defensive unit, releasing the attacking wing-back to provide offensive width.*

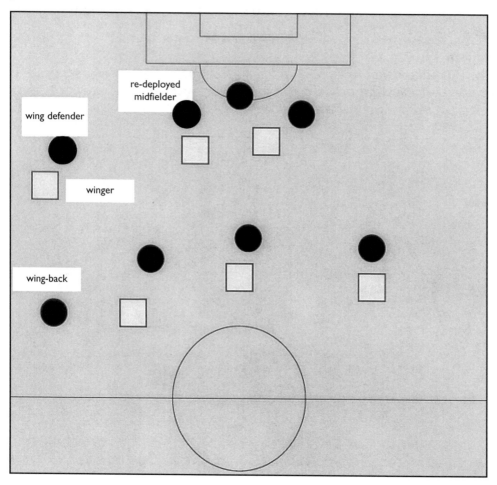

### 3.4 Should defenders show 'inside' or 'outside'?

As stated in the Introduction, defense in soccer, as in most invasion type games, is premised upon certain given principles. One of these is the denial of space to the attacking side. Another involves the protection of the central defensive area, thus forcing attacks into the less threatening outside sections of the field. Although both tactics make good defensive sense, the priority given to each in comparison to the other will dictate a team's overall defensive strategy. This could be expressed in terms of trying to force the opposition to play the ball wide and away from the defended goal, or alternatively, back into the middle areas where little space exists to develop potent attacks. Once the strategy has been decided upon, all the players in the team must adhere to it, attempting to make the opposition's play as predictable as possible.

## Showing the 'outside'

The strategy of showing the 'outside' involves channeling opposition attacks into the wide wing areas of the field, and away from the goal being defended. Defenders therefore often concede the pass into these areas, as possession there is generally considered less threatening than in the more central sectors. A team operating as such would thus deploy many players in the central areas when not in possession. A perceived strength of organizing the defensive unit in this way is that it forces the attack to go the 'long way round' the wing defenders or full-backs in order to achieve penetration and deliver a cross. If the defender is able and quick, it is quite a task for the forward to beat him on the outside and deliver a telling cross, often without breaking stride, into an area heavily fortified with defenders who specifically practice dealing with such situations. Additionally, if one of the goalkeeper's strengths is taking crosses, this makes the likelihood of a goal scoring opportunity even more remote (see Diagram 3.10).

## Diagram 3.10

*The attack is channeled into the less dangerous wider areas, due to defenders showing 'outside lines'.*

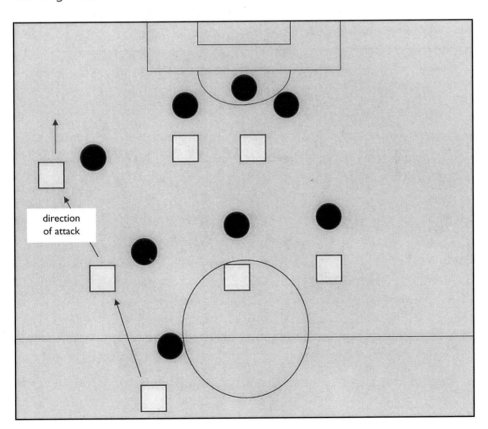

direction
of attack

## Showing the 'inside'

In contrast, a point of view that is sometimes heard claims that allowing attacks to develop down the wings leaves defenders in these positions frequently overexposed. If the wide attacking player is both quick and tricky, an early cross delivered from the goal line is a very potent attacking weapon. It is therefore believed that such deep defensive areas, and the defenders responsible for covering them, should be better protected, with the pass into such zones being denied. A favored way to achieve this is to force the opposition to pass or run with the ball into the central areas of the field. Such a tactic is based on the belief that by channeling the opposition into densely populated areas, space, and consequently time, to play the ball is denied. Additionally, by forcing the player in possession 'inside' he is also often compelled to use his weaker foot, thus lessening his capability on the ball which again increases the likelihood of the defensive side gaining possession. A final perceived advantage of utilizing such a tactic is that it generally keeps the play in front of the defensive unit. With many players occupying a limited space, penetration by the

**Diagram 3.11**

*The attacker in possession is forced to play the ball into the densely populated area in front of the defense as the pass forward into the wider wing area has been denied by defenders showing the 'inside line'.*

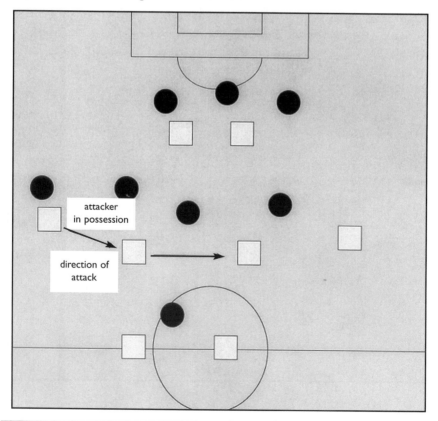

offensive side is difficult to achieve. Therefore, the areas behind the wing defenders from where dangerous crosses can be delivered are seldom reached by the attack, who in turn are forced to concentrate their play in the populated central areas which are easier to defend due to the lack of space available (see Diagram 3.11).

The effectiveness of both strategies has been repeatedly witnessed, hence no judgement is made about which is better. The key to efficiency of operation, as with most of the strategies and tactics discussed in this book, depends on acceptance and understanding by all the players involved, both as individuals and as a team. Such understanding comes with good practice.

### 3.5 Organizing the defense from corner kicks

In the modern game, corner kicks are considered potent offensive weapons which often lead to goal scoring chances. As such, many differing variations exist, all aimed at releasing an attacker in the penalty area who can then strike on goal. Due to their importance as attacking opportunities, two principal theories have evolved as to how best to negate their threat from a defensive viewpoint. In line with earlier defensive debates, this issue again centers on the adoption of a zonal or a man-to-man marking system.

**Defending corners using a zonal strategy**

**Diagram 3.12**
*In a zonal corner defense each man is given a certain space to cover, with the instruction to aggressively attack the ball if it enters his zone.*

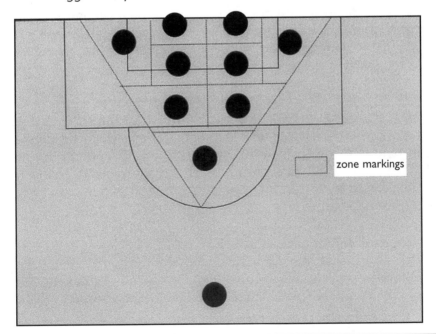

zone markings

This tactic, as its name suggests, is based on the understanding that individual defenders are allocated certain areas in the penalty box to cover. This usually takes the format of four defenders patrolling the edge of the 6 yard box, and another two being deployed a little further out at an imaginary 12 yard line. This leaves one man to deal with the half-clearances at the edge of the 18 yard box, and one left up-field. Additionally, two defenders are positioned by the posts. Diagram 3.12 clearly illustrates the organizational shape described.

The key to this defensive strategy is that the players must aggressively 'attack' the ball if it enters their zone. Thus, their starting positions should be towards the back of their allotted areas so that they are in a position to stride forward and meet the ball to clear it should it become playable in their respective zones. Some argue that one of the strengths of the system is the clear allocation of responsibility given to defenders in protecting their particular spaces. Supporters also point to the fact that if organized properly, the defender has more chance of beating an attacker to a header, as he is not distracted by the latter's movement and is left solely to concentrate on going to meet the ball. In theory, where one zone ends the other begins, therefore a large area in front of the goalkeeper is protected, as seen in Diagram 3.12.

### Defending corners using a man-to-man system

Detractors from the zonal system point out that although all areas are theoretically covered, in practice, difficulties exist. These primarily emerge when the ball drops or becomes playable on the lines dividing the zones. Confusion could arise as to whose responsibility it is to clear the ball in such instances. They further argue that the more concrete allocation of marking responsibilities given to defenders in a man-to-man system would circumvent such hesitation and confusion, which often proves costly. Each defender in such a system would be given an opponent to cover, with a further two defenders being deployed to cover the posts.

Within such a system, defenders usually try to interfere with the runs of attacking players by beating them to the space into which the latter wish to run. Consequently, the attackers are unable to get clear and 'clean' headers, as they must constantly jostle with their markers for position. Although this makes it difficult for the attacking side, they too use certain ploys to free a man. A favored tactic is to try to run the defenders into each other in an attempt to release a teammate at the far post for a free header.

### 3.6  How to counteract pace in attack

Perhaps the principal attribute that defenders fear most in forward opponents is pace. A forward's pace can very often destroy the most organized of defenses unless it is countered with equal speed. It becomes doubly difficult to defend against if the forward is running towards the defense with momentum, which requires the defenders to turn and begin their runs from almost a standing start in order to keep up and hopefully make a tackle. Coaches therefore, often instruct their defenders not to allow opponents to turn with the ball and 'get a run' at the defense. If this is achieved, the forward is forced to play the ball back into the midfield, or wide to the wings, thus considerably slowing the momentum of the attack and enabling the side not in possession to adopt a stronger defensive position by pulling more players behind the ball. Although basically this is sound advice, it is often proclaimed as a general comment or principle, and therefore not specifically part of an overall tactic or system of play. However, pace in attack can be negated through the deployment of certain strategies, almost all of which stress the need for depth in defense.

**Individual depth in defense**

**Diagram 3.13**
*The defender is in an ideal position to cover the run of the opposing forward, should he try to outrun the first defender into the advanced shaded area.*

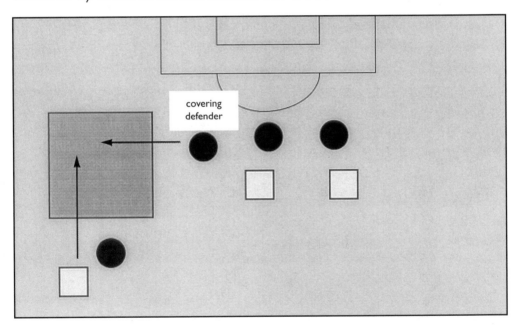

The basic principle of instilling depth in defense stems from the perceived need to supply cover to those challenging for the ball. Thus, if an attacker's threat emanates largely from his pace, the covering defender should be advised to adopt a little deeper position than normal. Consequently, if the attacker tries to outrun the first defender by relying on his principal attribute, the second defender needs to be in a position to cover his teammate should such a scenario occur. Diagram 3.13 illustrates the position of the covering defender in this regard, where his starting depth within the defensive unit enables him to control the situation.

Problems sometimes arise when the covering defender is too close to the first defender, thus not giving enough depth, and therefore allowing the speedy attacker the opportunity to outrun both in one burst. Additionally, if he has drifted too deep and is consequently too far away from the first defender to cover him, then he has become isolated from the defensive unit and risks exposure in a 1 v 1 situation should the first defender be beaten. His sense of positioning is crucial, while his powers of anticipation are equally vital if a successful defensive outcome is to be achieved.

### Collective depth in defense

If a team in general lacks pace in defense, relative to the level that it plays, one way that it can compensate for such a deficit is by electing to defend 'deep'. The objective of adopting such a strategy is not to allow any space behind the defense which could be exploited by attackers (see Diagram 3.14)

### Diagram 3.14

*If a team elects to defend deep, little space is left behind it (shaded area) for the offensive side to exploit, thus making penetration difficult.*

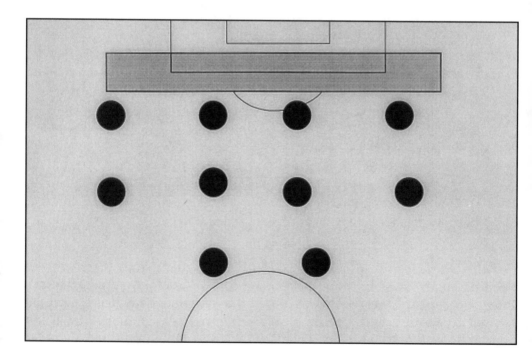

By defending deep, the pass over the defense to speedy forwards running through is generally negated, as the space into which the ball would be played is occupied by defenders. Although they can still construct lateral runs across the face of the defense which can sometimes prove problematic, the penetrating forward runs characteristic of quick forwards are much less in evidence, thus the offensive threat is decreased. Alternatively, in order to penetrate such a defense, the attacking side has to try to pass through, as opposed to over it, which is generally much more difficult. However, if such a defensive strategy is adopted, it is imperative that the whole team and not only the defensive unit adhere to it. This is a very important point, because if spaces exist between the defense and the midfield, these can be exploited by deep lying forwards, while additionally, passes could easily reach the feet of the forwards causing considerable problems. Although the principle of adopting such a defensive strategy rests on the premise of denying space to opponents behind the defense, it is also important for the midfield to patrol the area in front of it, with the forwards doing likewise to the midfield. Thus, defending deep becomes a strategy for the team, not just the defensive unit.

Although defending deeply as a team is a very effective defensive strategy, problems arise when possession is won. When the aforementioned occurs, a quick incisive attack is often difficult to mount as most of the players are in deep defending positions. This, in turn, allows the opposition time to re-group and organize its own defense before the attack generates the width and momentum it needs to achieve penetration. A further discussion of this issue is embarked upon in Chapter 7, although suffice to say that one of the considered drawbacks of defending deep is the problem faced in launching an effective attack when the ball is won.

Chapter 4
# THE ONE FORWARD SYSTEM

**4.1 Description and definition**
**4.2 The role of the forward within the system**
**4.3 The role of the two attacking midfielders within the system**
**4.4 The advantages and disadvantages of the system**

## 4.1 Description and definition

The one forward system is also known as the 'pyramid' or 'Christmas tree' formation, which gives a clear indication of its shape. Within it, one forward is supported by two advanced midfielders, who in turn can be supported by a three man midfield and a four man defense. If the second midfield tier comprises four, then a three man defense is naturally utilized (see Diagram 4.1).

**Diagram 4.1**
*The one forward or pyramid formation, comprising one orthodox forward, two advanced midfielders, 3 orthodox midfielders and four defenders.*

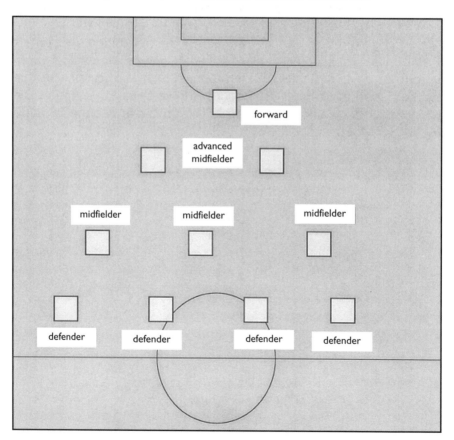

## 4.2  The role of the forward within the system

One of the principal duties of the forward in this type of system, once he has received the ball, is to keep possession until support arrives, usually from the attacking midfielders. He thus has an isolated role, as he is often used as a target man who his teammates look to find with early forward passes. As befits such a role, much of his time is spent facing his own goal, shielding the ball when in possession in order to give time for supporting teammates to arrive and then to bring them into the play. He is, almost without exception, the most spatially advanced player in the team, therefore the direction of his passes are generally square or back to supporting teammates. Once this has been achieved, he should then concentrate on getting into the opponents' penalty box in anticipation of a cross or pass.

The runs he makes in order to find space to receive the ball are of critical importance to his game. As he can rarely be expected to chase balls played over the defense, most of the passes played to him should be to his feet or at a comfortable, controllable height. In order that a defender not be given the opportunity to intercept such passes, he must often move away from the center areas at an angle away from the opponent's goal to find the space desired (see Diagram 4.2).

In order that the forward achieves maximum effectiveness within the system, he should not run too wide into the wing positions to accept the ball, however tempting the greater spaces there might be. The reasons for this are principally twofold. Firstly, by receiving the ball wide on the wing, the arriving support can only come from one direction (from his inside), thus making the attack predictable and simple to defend against. Secondly, by taking up such a position, he has, to all intents and purposes, taken himself out of the second phase of the attack, as the length of his run into the box has now increased considerably. Furthermore, if his run has taken him wide onto the wing, the supporting players now lack a central offensive focus and target through which to continue and develop the attack. Consequently, they are often forced to pass square or back, losing momentum.

Conversely, by restricting his runs to within a central 30 yard channel (see Diagram 4.2), he can bring teammates from his left or right into play, and is able to maintain his role as a central striker by making a secondary run into the penalty box in anticipation of meeting a cross or receiving a second pass. The type of run into the box expected of forwards is discussed at length in Chapter 5.

## 4.3  The role of the two attacking midfielders

The respective roles of the two attacking midfielders are very similar in that, as a principal function, they are expected to give early support to the forward once he is in possession. They generally operate in the space between the forward and the orthodox midfield unit, and have a considerable degree of freedom within the constraints of the formation. Although they are not restricted to zones, it is usual that one will favor the right side, and the other the left.

### Diagram 4.2
*Forward runs involve moving wide and away from the opponents' goal. The forward's runs should remain within a given channel for maximum effectiveness.*

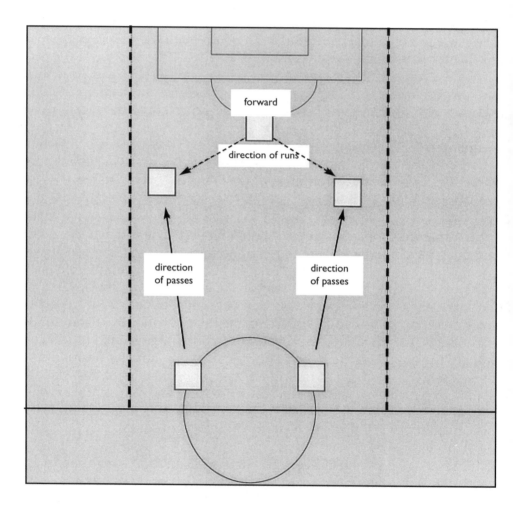

The freedom of the two attacking midfielders often makes them potent offensive weapons, who, as well as feeding the central striker, should also be in positions to receive passes from him to shoot at goal. They are also often expected to provide width to the attack, particularly if the second midfield tier only comprises of three players. Their role in many ways mirrors that of the 'man in the hole', but is often considered more difficult. This is due to their limited forward passing options (they usually only have one teammate ahead of them), and to the fact that two of them are often operating in close proximity. The situation is exacerbated by their need not to be too close to the forward too early, thus drawing more defenders towards him and cutting down his space, which the attack needs if it is to further develop. To prevent such a situation from occurring, the attacking midfielders need to concentrate on making two specific kinds of runs, one to receive the ball in a deeper position, and the other to penetrate the defense.

As shown in Diagram 4.3, to receive the ball from the central striker the attacking midfielders should respect the spaces both between themselves and the central striker and also between each other, and alternatively try to find room through short lateral or angled diagonal runs. Such an angle preserves the room the central striker needs to work in, while not drawing any more defenders towards him (see Diagram 4.3).

## Diagram 4.3
*The attacking midfielders should embark on lateral or diagonal runs to find space, and not encroach on that of the central striker i.e. the darker shaded area.*

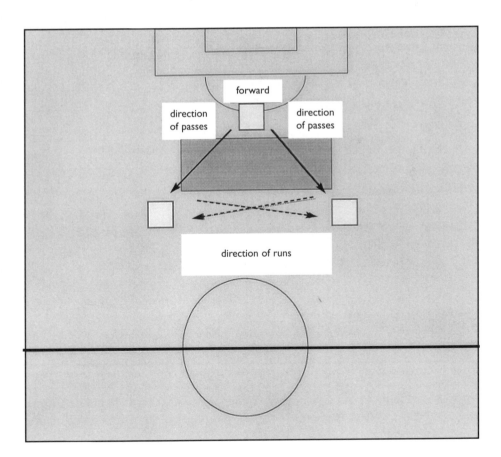

Additionally, the attacking midfielders should on occasions embark on runs in advance of the central striker to receive a penetrating pass from another midfielder once the ball has been laid back from the aforementioned central striker. Very often this is an effective ploy as the defense has difficulty in picking up opponents who run from deeper positions. Furthermore, as the system only employs one orthodox forward, such runs greatly increase the attacking capability of the team (see Diagram 4.4).

**Diagram 4.4**
*The attacking midfielder has run from a deeper position to receive a through pass from another midfielder after the ball has been laid back by the central striker.*

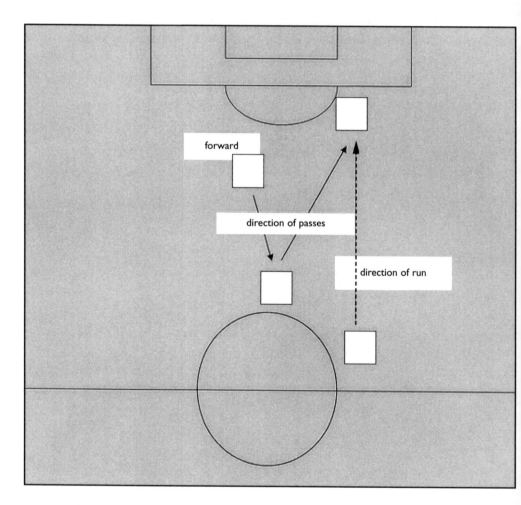

## 4.4 The advantages and disadvantages of the system

The main advantage of the system is that the midfield area should be well contested due to the large number of players stationed there. Additionally, if the midfielders are constantly interchanging positions, defenders are faced with considerable problems regarding who to pick up. This is especially so if penetrating runs in advance of the central striker are a systematic and regular feature of the game plan.

Conversely, one of the principal weaknesses of the system is often seen as its consistent lack of penetration, often due to the isolation of the central striker and the inability of the midfield to give him early support. The system additionally is heavily reliant on the ability of the central striker to hold the ball, which if not forthcoming, is liable to prove the strategy largely ineffective. A further concern with the system emanates from its lack of natural early width. Although the attacking midfielders or wide players in the second midfield unit could provide some width in this respect, if they are not in a position early enough to receive the ball to cross it, the defensive side will have time to organize and any attacking momentum will be lost.

# Chapter 5
# THE TWO FORWARD SYSTEM

**5.1 Description and definition**
**5.2 The role of the two central strikers within the system**
Offensive responsibilities
Defensive responsibilities
**5.3 Advantages and disadvantages of the system**

### 5.1. Description and definition

A formation incorporating two central strikers is the most common in modern soccer, and is evident in both the 4-4-2 and 3-5-2 tactical systems. Generally, these striking partnerships involve complementary players, comprising a tall robust target figure, and a smaller, quicker teammate, playing 'off' the former. The first is adept at the aerial game and is able to hold the ball well to feed supporting teammates, while the second is usually very skilful and speedy, capable of cleverly creating goal scoring opportunities for others as well as converting chances himself. The complementary nature of their relationship is often considered an advantage, as many and varied problems are posed to defenders if their respective strengths are continuously and alternately utilized.

### 5.2 The role of the two central strikers within the system

The role of the two strikers, who operate almost exclusively in central areas, can be divided between their offensive and defensive duties. Although undoubtedly their principal responsibility within the team is to score goals and to engineer goal scoring opportunities for others, thus providing an attacking fulcrum to the offense, they are also considered to be the first line of defense. Consequently, their duties in this regard should be made clear and emphasized as an integral part of their respective roles.

### Offensive responsibilities

Similar to the runs required by the single striker within the 'Christmas tree' formation discussed in Chapter 4, the forwards within this system should also, in general, restrict their movement to a central channel to receive the ball. Thus, they would remain a central focus for the attack as it develops a second phase, and be able to reach the penalty box to meet anticipated crosses from the wide flank players or wingers.

In addition to angling their runs away from defenders to receive the ball, a feature of their game should be their understanding of who should make which run where in order to find space to receive the ball in a heavily congested area. The forwards should switch positions often, running laterally across each other to shake off their markers (see Diagram 5.1).

**Diagram 5.1**

*The strikers should constantly interchange or switch positions to find space, while generally remaining within a central channel.*

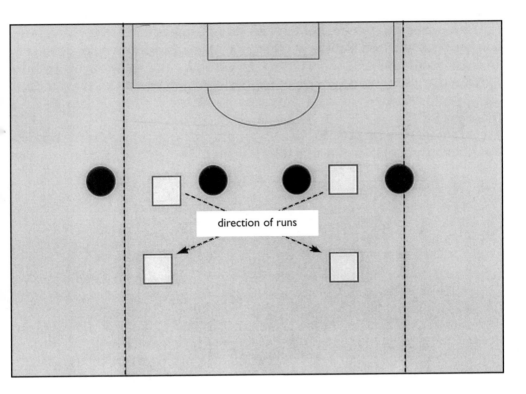

direction of runs

In order to introduce an element of unpredictability into their play, at least one of the forwards should, on occasion, attempt to run through the defense in anticipation of a longer pass played over or through it. As one forward comes short on an angled run pulling a defender with him, the other should embark on a longer one utilizing the space created behind the aforementioned defender (see Diagram 5.2).

Such runs through the defense into the space beyond it are often seen either very early or much later in games. The first is usually an attempt to catch defenders 'cold', while they are still finding their collective way into the game. Similarly, the second is also used as a surprise tactic; having come short on angled runs to passes played to feet during the early phases of the game, by suddenly and unpredictably varying the run to one described above (see Diagram 5.2), the element of surprise can often lead to an opportunity for the forward to strike at goal.

The strikers should work as a pair as much as possible, which necessitates that they remain within a certain distance of each other throughout the game. If a distance of 30 yards or less is not maintained, then the strikers become isolated from each other, decreasing their individual and collective effectiveness. Furthermore, a distance greater than 30 yards assumes that a wide wing position has been adopted by at least one of the forwards, which denies the attack a central focus, while additionally occupying space the wide players wish to use to run at the wing defenders or full-backs. Alternately, by keeping in close

**Diagram 5.2**
*The ball is played into the space behind the defender who is marking the first forward for the on-running second forward.*

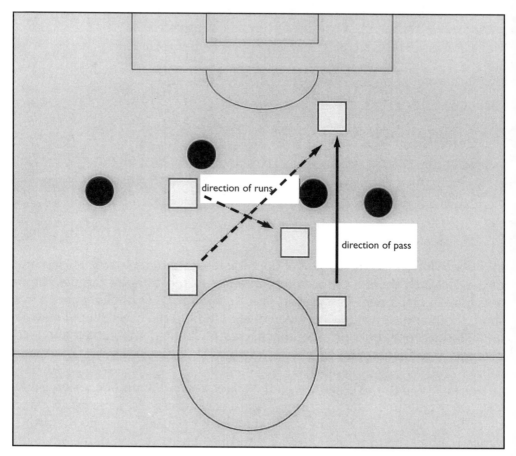

proximity to each other, they are able to play off and feed each other, giving the team a more effective cutting edge.

Again, echoing the role of the forward in the 'Christmas tree' formation, a favored option for the forwards when in possession should be to pass to the wider flank players before circling to run into the penalty box to meet an anticipated cross. Such runs, however, should not be made on an ad-hoc basis, but as a pair, with each aware of the other's movements. More specifically on this point, as illustrated in Diagram 5.3, if the ball is delivered from an advanced wide area, 'high' up the field, one forward should endeavor to run hard to reach the space just in front of the near post as the ball is crossed. Conversely, and simultaneously, the other should loop his run around to arrive at the far post in anticipation of the ball being delivered into that area.

**Diagram 5.3**
*As the ball is crossed from the wing, the forwards should be engaged in complimentary runs; one to the near post and one to the far post.*

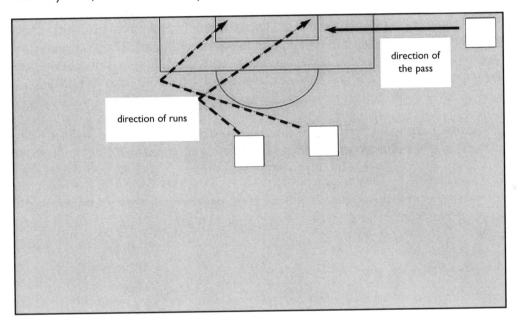

The logic behind the run to the near post rests on the assumption that the cross will be under-hit, and will not clear the first defender located at the near post, as is often the case. One of the forwards must expect such an occurrence and beat the defender and the goalkeeper to the space just in front of the near post and then attempt to deflect the ball goalwards. Naturally, this must be a quick and aggressive run, as defenders are aware of the need to meet the ball first and of the vulnerability of this area in particular.

Alternatively, the far post run is made on the assumption that a longer cross will be hit into this area. This is often a very effective position to take up, as defenders are sometimes caught watching the ball and are unaware when forwards pull away into the space just beyond the far post. If the ball correspondingly arrives, the defenders are caught out of position, and a good goal scoring opportunity for the forward is available.

Although such runs are common in modern soccer, their relevance and effectiveness depends entirely on the ball being crossed from an advanced wing area; for example, after a winger has beaten his full-back on the outside. Conversely, when the wide attacker in possession has been forced 'inside', with the play being kept generally in front of the defense, a different kind of run is expected from the forwards.

As illustrated in Diagram 5.4, if the winger in possession is forced inside, the forwards should embark on angled runs behind the defense, inviting the pass between the defenders. In order to increase the effectiveness of such movement, the forward nearest the ball should move laterally away from the ball-carrier dragging his defender, to a certain extent, with him. The space has now been created for a penetrating pass between the full-back and the central defender to the on-running forward to shoot at goal (see Diagram 5.4).

## Diagram 5.4

*If the flank attacker cuts inside, one attacker should try to draw the nearest center-back out of position to allow a penetrating pass to the on-running second forward.*

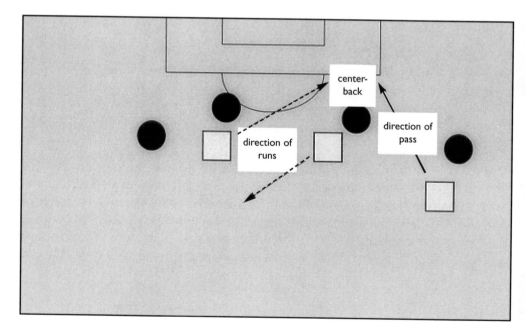

## Defensive responsibilities

The defensive duties of the forwards in such a system are often considerable, as they are generally expected to occupy the attention of all the opposing defenders, be they three or four in number. While the forwards could logically be expected to contain a three man defense by not allowing them time and space to play accurate passes forward with relative ease, when four defenders are present a little more strategic thinking and planning is necessary.

In order to deny a four man defense comfortable possession, the forwards should position themselves between a full-back and a central defender on each side, inhibiting distribution of the ball from the goalkeeper to any one individual defender (see Diagram 5.5). Defenders, in turn, attempt to circumvent this ploy by spreading across the width of the field, thus giving the forwards a much greater area to cover. If this is done early and quickly enough once the goalkeeper is in possession of the ball, they are usually able to play the ball out of defense despite the best efforts of the two forwards to the contrary. Nevertheless, a tactic exists which can maximize the likelihood of the forwards regaining possession through their defensive work. This involves each forward initially covering a full-back ensuring that the latter will not gain possession,

## Diagram 5.5
*The two forwards position themselves between a central defender and a full-back to inhibit any one defender from gaining time and space in possession.*

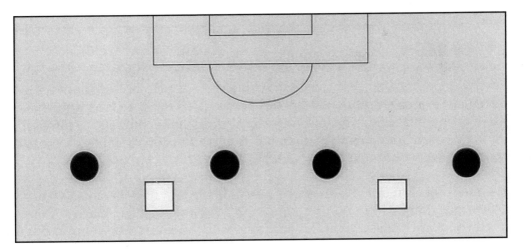

while allowing or even encouraging the center-backs to receive the ball from the goalkeeper. Such a move is based on the premise that center-backs are often far less comfortable in possession than full-backs. Consequently, when pressure is then applied to the center-back in possession, either through an advancing midfielder or the forwards closing in from the wings, a quality forward pass is much less likely to be delivered (see Diagram 5.6).

**Diagram 5.6**
*Pressure is applied to the center-back in possession from an advanced midfield player and/or from the forwards closing in from the wings.*

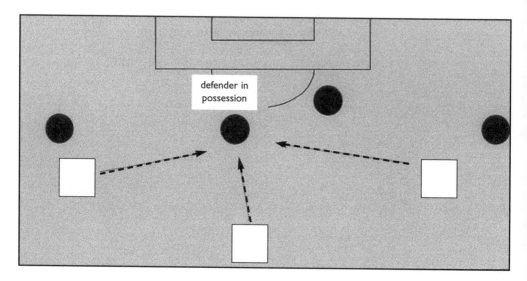

## 5.3 Advantages and disadvantages of the system

One of the main advantages of the system is the early support offered to the forward in possession, principally from his striking partner. Additionally, by operating as a pair, and understanding each other's roles, a clever and effective working relationship between the forwards is sometimes apt to develop, through which they are able to create goal scoring opportunities for each other.

The main criticism levied against the system is the lack of evident early natural forward width, which must be supplied by the wing midfield players. This is often overcome however, by the dual role of such players who tend to position themselves as midfielders when defending, but as wingers when attacking. The key to the role switch lies in anticipation of when and where the ball will be won, and moving early to support the forward players in advanced upfield positions.

# Chapter 6
# THE THREE FORWARD SYSTEM

**6.1 Description and definition**
**6.2 The role of the two central strikers when playing with a winger**
**6.3 The role of the winger**
**6.4 Advantages and disadvantages of playing with a winger**
**6.5 The three central striker system**
        Note: The 4-2-4 system

## 6.1 Description and definition

The system incorporating three forwards is usually considered to include two central strikers and a winger, within a 4-3-3 formation. The other principal variant on the theme is that which includes three central strikers. This latter pattern has become a rare sight in the modern game as many coaches perceive it not structured enough in an attacking sense. Consequently, although a brief analysis of it will be made, this chapter will chiefly focus on the formation inclusive of an orthodox winger as the third forward (see Diagram 6.1).

**Diagram 6.1**
*A 4-3-3 formation including two central strikers and a winger.*

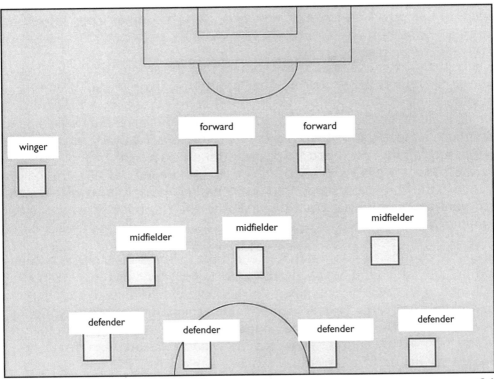

## 6.2 The role of the two central strikers when playing with a winger

The respective roles of the two central strikers playing together has been largely covered in the previous chapter. The type of runs expected from them, the areas of the field in which they should operate, the distance that should exist between them and the complimentary nature of a successful striking partnership are equally applicable to them when operating with or without a winger.

Differences do exist however, none more so than in the pattern of ball distribution expected from the central strikers. Generally speaking, the earlier the ball is given to the winger the more momentum he can build to run at his fullback. It is the primary aim of the winger to beat his defender, usually a fullback, and to cross accurately from the outside spaces that exist behind the defense. Therefore, when playing with a winger, the strikers should try to adopt a more lateral passing game, looking to give the ball to him as a primary option instead of a deeper lying midfield player. Although this is not always possible, the concept of trying to achieve early width must remain high in the distribution priorities of the centrally positioned forwards.

Once the winger is in possession of the ball, the forwards should make every effort to undertake penetrating angled runs into the opposing penalty box to arrive simultaneously with the ball. As wingers are often very direct, speedy players, the strikers must work hard to reach this destination in time, in order to meet the anticipated cross. The runs undertaken by the strikers into the box in this regard should be similar to those already discussed in the previous chapter, with one attacking the near post area, while the other loops his run to arrive at the far post (see Diagram 5.3).

It is important to remember in this context that the strikers, as a rule, should not go to support the winger by running into the space ahead of him for a pass up the line. Although the likelihood of completing such a pass is high, which results in possession being maintained in a more advanced up-field position, such a move should be avoided for two reasons. Firstly, by receiving the ball in such a wide area, often facing away from the goal, the options available to the striker to further develop the attack are limited. Usually, the ball is passed back from such a position, and although possession is maintained, offensive momentum has been lost enabling the defensive side time to re-group and re-organize.

Secondly, by running into the space behind the full-back the striker is occupying the area which the winger needs to use to beat his man, thus leaving the only option for the winger in possession a square or back pass to a supporting midfielder. Again, attacking momentum has been lost. In contrast, any support play in this situation should come from a deeper midfield player, with the forwards dragging defenders away from the winger, isolating him in a contest against the full-back with plenty of space to work in (see Diagram 6.2).

## Diagram 6.2

*Central strikers should attempt to drag defenders away from the winger thus vacating the space behind the full-back (shaded area). Support for the winger should come from the trailing midfielder.*

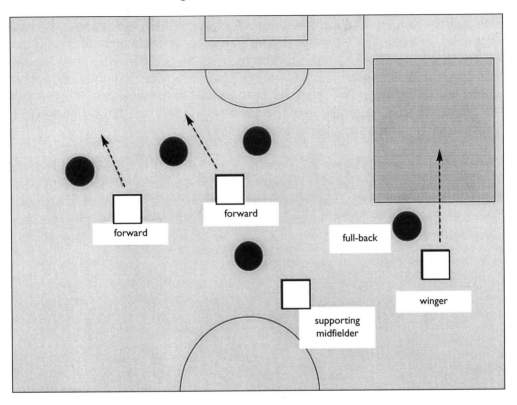

### 6.3 The role of the winger

The role of the winger is principally to provide offensive width to the team. In many ways therefore, his role is limited to providing early accurate crosses, preferably with pace, into the opposition's penalty area. He should have numerous feints and moves with which to beat his opponent, both on the 'outside' and the 'inside', and be unpredictable in this aspect of his play. The 'outside' in this context refers to the area between the full-back and the side line, while alternately the 'inside' refers to the infield area encroaching on the more central spaces.

It would be remiss here to paint a picture in which the winger is only considered to be an offensive threat. In most cases, when possession has been lost, wingers are expected to shuttle back assuming almost a midfield role until the ball is won again. Thus, very often, a team formation is altered from a 4-3-3 to a 4-4-2 and back again depending on who has possession. Additionally, a winger is sometimes used to negate the threat of a particularly offensively minded full-back. In this context, by preoccupying such an opponent in a defensive capacity, a winger can restrict the fullback's opportunities to move forward, thus performing a useful defensive function for the team.

### 6.4 Advantages and disadvantages of playing with a winger

The main advantage of playing with a winger in the team formation is the natural early forward width provided. The transition from defense to attack can be easily and quickly accomplished by feeding the winger, who then usually embarks on a very positive and direct objective. Consequently, opposing teams are loath to commit many midfielders and hardly any defenders to join an attack, as they generally fear the pace of wingers on the counter-attack which could leave them vulnerable defensively.

The disadvantage of playing with a winger is that he is heavily dependent on the service from others, and is therefore sometimes liable to spend long periods with little involvement in the game. Furthermore, the logistics of his position and role dictate that if he seeks the ball by moving infield or coming very deep to receive it, he ceases, by and large, to be an effective offensive threat.

### 6.5 The three central striker system

**Diagram 6.3**
*A 4-3-3 formation utilizing three central strikers.*

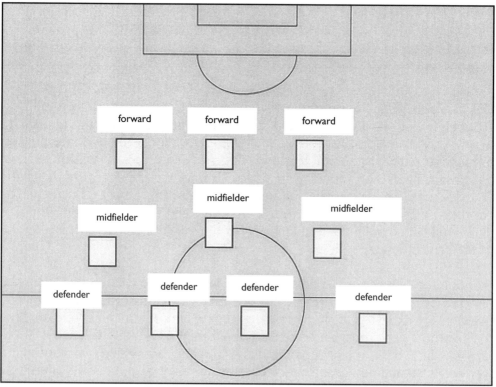

The three central striker system, as illustrated in Diagram 6.3, is a rarely seen formation in the modern game. In many ways it is a very attacking arrangement, but a very difficult one to implement correctly; a realization which has probably contributed to its decline. The strength of the system is unsurprisingly viewed as its central striking capability, while it additionally ought to provide substantial attacking width, with one of the strikers constantly breaking into wide wing positions to receive the ball. The formation possesses good forward support, and with the strikers constantly inter-changing their positions, zone defenders in particular are faced with many problems.

Critics, however, have argued that such a system falls short of effectiveness on two major fronts. Firstly, that the offensive width produced is not consistent, and is likely to vanish as quickly as it appears, thus making it difficult to establish an offensive pattern of play. Secondly, it is perceived that many of the runs embarked upon by the strikers are often duplicated by each other, while not enough forward depth is evident in the formation. Indeed, the difficulty inherent in coordinating the work of three strikers in the central channel of the field has resulted in the decline of this variation of the three man forward system.

### Note: The 4-2-4 system

It is acknowledged that a major offensive system not covered specifically in this book is the 4-2-4, utilizing four forwards incorporating two wingers. However, the role of the two central strikers within the system has been covered in Chapter 5, while Chapter 6 has discussed at length the role of the winger. Consequently, in order to avoid repetition, suffice to say that a reading of both chapters covers the main issues inherent within a 4-2-4 system, although not specifically within the context of that formation.

The main advantage of the 4-2-4 system is the availability of early wide support to the central strikers from both wings. The opposing defense should consequently always be stretched, unless a third central defender is deployed as a covering player, which correspondingly weakens the midfield. Additionally, having two wingers restricts the attacking capabilities of both opposing fullbacks, as neither is loath to neglect his defensive marking duties to join the offense.

Conversely, the principal weakness of the system lies in the limited capability of its 2 man midfield, which very often finds itself outnumbered. If the midfield are unable to provide the attacking wingers with adequate possession, the latter are prone to be under-involved, and largely cease to become a threat. Indeed, it was in response to such a scenario that the 4-4-2 formation evolved, which gave greater defensive and midfield solidarity by deploying the flank players a little deeper. However, as stated earlier, this is prone to immediate transformation to a 4-2-4 once possession has been won.

Chapter 7
# OFFENSIVE/ATTACKING ISSUES

## 7.1 Introduction
The aim of this chapter is to highlight and  discuss three contrasting issues in offensive play. The first involves a discussion of the principal areas where goals are scored from, and how attacking players should run into such zones. The second examines the role of the advanced midfield player, or the 'man in the hole', a position which has become increasingly fashionable in the recent past. Finally, the third contains some suggested ways to create goal scoring opportunities from corners.

## 7.2 Where goals are scored from
Research has demonstrated that 'prime scoring areas' exist, from where a particularly high percentage of goals are scored (Hughes, 1990). These involve the spaces at, and just ahead of, the near post, and at, and just behind, the far post. This is particularly true of the far post area, where it has been demonstrated that over 20% of all goals are scored (see Diagram 7.1).

**Diagram 7.1**
*If an attack is developing on the offensive team's right wing, the prime scoring areas become the spaces just beyond the near and far posts (shaded areas).*

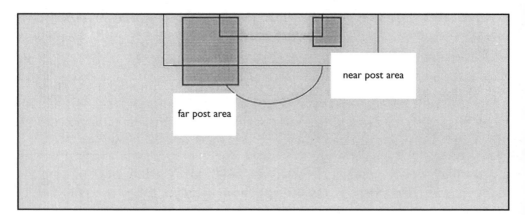

near post area

far post area

The runs made by the forwards into these contrasting spaces are very different in their nature, manner and intensity. As discussed in Chapter 5, the run made to the near post must be quick and aggressive to beat the defender to the ball in anticipation of a low cross or a cross being under-hit. In contrast, the run made to the space beyond the far post is often much less conspicuous, as the forward is attempting to find space behind the defender. In order to encourage this, players are often told to 'peel off the defender's shoulder' whose attention has been momentarily distracted by watching the ball. The aim here is to position oneself where the defender cannot watch both the forward and the ball simultaneously, while maintaining his necessary position between the forward and the goal (see Diagram 7.2).

## Diagram 7.2

*If the attacking side has possession on their right, the attacker should pull away from the outside shoulder of his defender on a curved run taking him into the prime scoring area (shaded).*

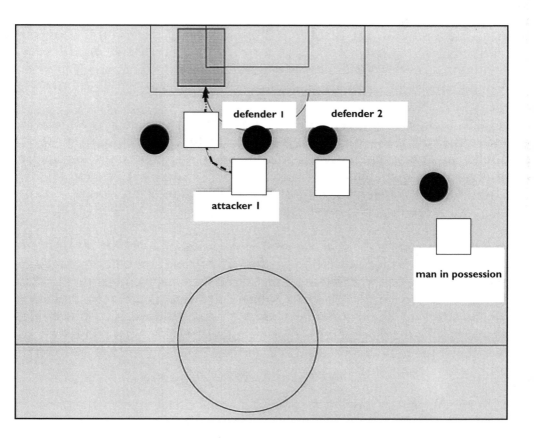

Diagram 7.2 clearly illustrates the dilemma facing defenders (particularly defender 1) in this situation who are trying to hold a defensive line, mark a forward and watch the ball simultaneously. The attacker (attacker 1) meanwhile attempts to find space between defenders by pulling away from his marker (defender 1) on a curved, or even backward, run taking him into the prime scoring area beyond the far post into where the ball could be delivered (see Diagram 7.2). The forward should delay this run into the space beyond the defender until the last moment and make it as inconspicuous as possible, because if he moves too soon, and too blatantly, he may well attract the attention of the defender he is trying to escape.

### 7.3 The role of the 'man in the hole'

The growth in popularity of positioning a player in the area between the traditional midfield and forward units has been considerable over the past few years. Generally, he is expected to support two forwards (see Diagrams 7.3[a] and 7.3[b]), although in very recent times, withdrawing one of the two central strikers to occupy the role, enabling the team to maintain greater defensive and midfield solidarity with 4 players stationed in each unit has become increasingly popular (see Diagram 7.3[c]). Whichever formation is used, the player deployed in the 'hole' is often a creative and talented individual, who, although capable of scoring goals himself, is generally more adept at engineering opportunities for others.

His effectiveness is, in part, attributable to defensive uncertainty as to who should mark him, as central defenders are wary to follow him to such a deep position as it compromises their covering role. Although defenses are capable of implementing strategies to compensate for his presence, as discussed in Chapter 3, they often involve considerable disruption of their original game plan, which can itself be problematic.

In order to maximize the effectiveness of this critical position, the player occupying it should be fed possession as often as possible and be encouraged to actively seek the ball. The defense is thus faced with many problems as to how to deal with him early in the game, which could lead to profitable hesitation for the attacking side. Furthermore, through gaining possession in a central attacking area, the defense is usually drawn towards him, allowing his forward teammates the opportunity to 'pull off' the respective shoulders of the defenders into dangerous areas.

Such complimentary forward runs are vital to the effectiveness of the player in the 'hole', as they should provide his most preferred passing option when in possession. If playing behind two forwards, he could expect both forwards to embark on such curved runs (see Diagram 7.4), or alternately, just one. In the case of the latter scenario, the other forward should face the player in possession, be prepared to play a wall pass or 'one-two' with him, keeping the defense focused on a central attacking point before threading or lifting his second pass into the path of the forward who has 'pulled off' the shoulder of a defender into a prime scoring area (see Diagram 7.5). Naturally, good practice and understanding of each other's roles are vital in the effective execution of such a play.

In order to be able to work effectively in tandem with his forward teammate(s), it is imperative that the 'man in the hole' respects the space between them, particularly if the latter's offensive threat comes from his passing abilities. As discussed in Chapter 4, and specifically illustrated in Diagram 4.3, this deeper attacker should embark on lateral runs to find space in which to receive the ball. He should therefore not encroach on the space of his forwards, as by doing so he would inevitably drag more defenders towards the ball carrier. Furthermore, by embarking on such lateral movements he is assured of being in a position to receive the ball from his forwards as he has not over-run the play.

**Diagram 7.3(a)**
*The position of the 'man in the hole' between the forward(s) and the midfield is evident if playing with two or one orthodox forwards.*

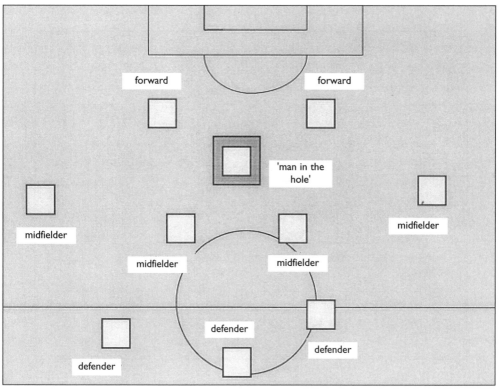

## Diagram 7.3 (b)

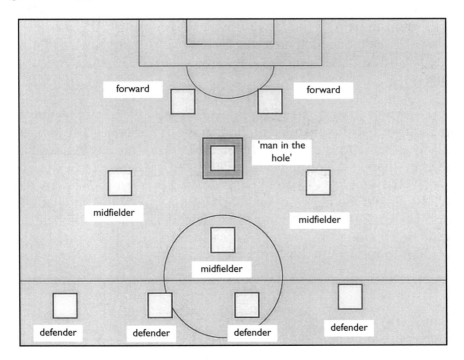

## Diagram 7.3 (c)

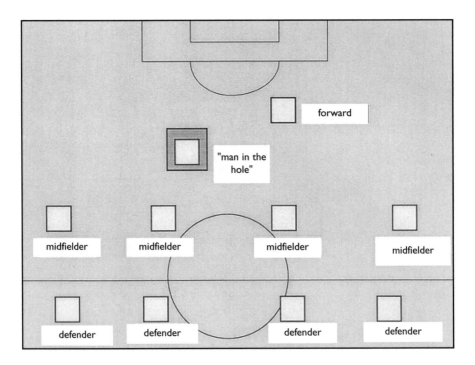

### Diagram 7.4
*The preferred passing option of the 'man in the hole' should be to forward team-mates pulling off the shoulders of defenders into scoring positions.*

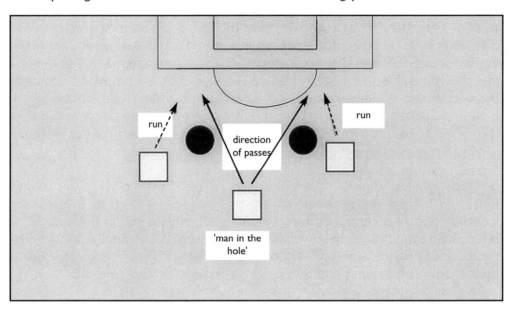

### Diagram 7.5
*If a wall pass is played with one forward, the defense's concentration often becomes fixated on the ball, allowing a second 'through' pass to be made to the other forward running into a prime scoring area.*

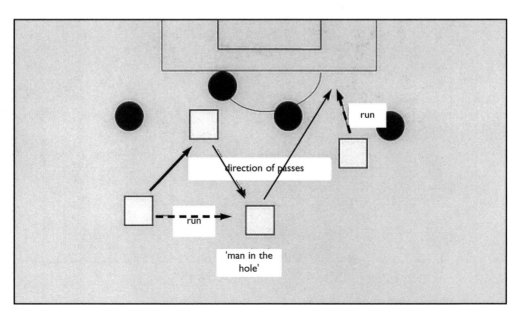

As mentioned in Chapter 3, sometimes the danger emanating from the player occupying the 'hole' comes from his ability to run into advanced positions behind the defense himself, rather than passing the ball there for others. This type of player poses a different kind of threat altogether, as his runs are difficult for defenders to pick up. He thus tries to exploit the spaces between defenders by creating confusion as to who should take responsibility for marking him, and, through his run, encourages the longer pass over the defense into the vulnerable space behind it (see Diagram 7.6). Such runs are similar to those expected of the two attacking midfield players in the 'Christmas tree' formation described in Chapter 4. His role is made even more effective if one of the forwards adopts a little deeper position, thus pulling a defender with him leaving the space behind into which the run can be made.

Being designated to play in the 'hole' need not restrict this player's role to only that area behind the more advanced forwards, particularly in a formation incorporating two central strikers. Within such a team shape not only is he often encouraged to run in advance of the forwards, but also to drift into wider positions to provide offensive width. Consequently, his role has far less limitations than most, making him an elusive opponent, difficult to mark.

**Diagram 7.6**
*By pulling one of the defenders into a deeper position, the space is created where the 'man in the hole' can run to receive a penetrating pass.*

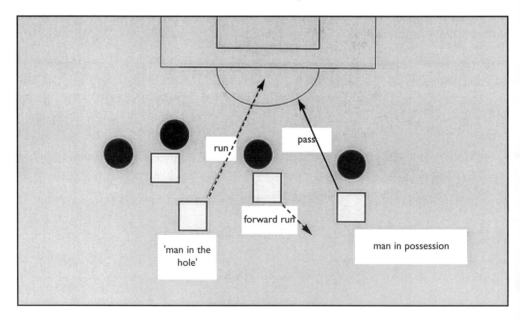

## 7.4 Attacking corner kicks

Although there is an infinite variety of tactics utilized at corner kicks in an attempt to engineer a clean strike on goal, we thought it appropriate to illustrate three of our particular favorites here. Needless to say there was limited agreement as to the most effective!

### The near post corner

### Diagram 7.7
*The ball is played into the near post area to be flicked on to late arriving teammates in the middle and far post regions.*

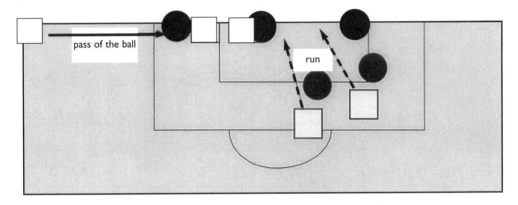

By placing a tall player at the near post, the aim is to deliver the ball into that area, so he is able to flick it on across the face of the goal. It is anticipated that the flick will then be met by either one of two teammates who are running through toward the center and the far post areas respectively. This tactic is a particularly difficult one to defend against because if the delivery from the corner is accurate, an effective flick on from the near post is just as likely to come from defenders trying to clear the ball as the attacker.

More often than not, the defending team will station a player in front as well as behind the attacker in this situation in an attempt to prevent the flick on. However, if the attacker takes a more forward position initially, and then backs up to the near post area as the ball is delivered, the defender in front is often taken out of the play. Additionally, as a result of such a move, the forward is generally also able to flick on a ball entering the area at a lower trajectory than would have been possible if a defender was still stationed immediately in front of him.

One of the principal reasons why this ploy is so effective is that it draws the goalkeeper to the near post area, catching him out of position when the ball is flicked on to the central or far post areas. Additionally, by focusing the concentration of defenders at the near post when the ball is delivered, they are prone to be caught ball-watching rather than following their allotted forwards as the latter run into central and far post scoring positions (see Diagram 7.7).

### The out-swinging near post corner

### Diagram 7.8
*The space on the corner of the six-yard box is deliberately left vacant. The ball is delivered into the area to be met by an aggressively running forward who must beat his defender to the ball.*

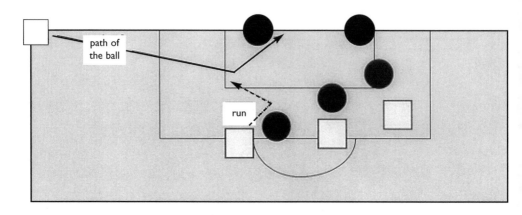

As opposed to delivering the ball to a player already in position, as in the conventional near post corner, the out-swinging near post corner involves delivery of the ball into a space which has been deliberately left vacant. The ball here is curled outwards towards the near corner of the six-yard box to be met by a teammate making a specific and well timed run into that area. Although naturally the accuracy of delivery is important, of greater significance here is the need for the forward to get in front of the defender, beating him to the space and the ball. In order to maximize the likelihood of doing this, the forward should initially endeavor to drag his defender away from the space before running into it, or attacking it, aggressively (see Diagram 7.8).

### The far post short corner
As its name suggests, this tactic involves initially playing the ball back and short to a teammate who in turn delivers it to the far post area to a forward in space. The ploy is premised on the assumption that the defense will move out as the ball is played back to the edge of the 18 yard box to a player who has run from a deeper position. The ball should then be delivered by this player immediately, if possible, into the space created between the advancing defensive line and the goalkeeper. The forwards correspondingly should move out with the

defenders, lest they be caught offside, leaving a deeper lying teammate, or one who has curved his run around to the far post area to arrive simultaneously with the ball (see Diagram 7.9).

### Diagram 7.9
*The ball is played back and consequently delivered immediately into the space between the advancing defense and the goalkeeper to a forward running from a deeper position, thus ensuring that he is not offside.*

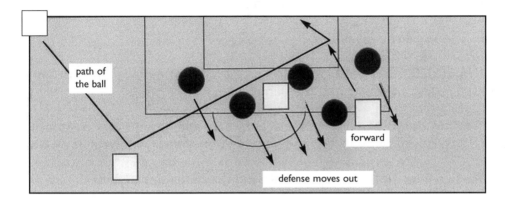

# GLOSSARY

**Attacking the ball:** Advancing positively to meet the ball.

**Attacking the space:** Aggressively running into a space with the ball or to meet an anticipated pass.

**Ball watching:** A defender's tendency to watch the ball while allowing a forward to find space behind and beyond him.

**Box:** The 18 yard penalty box.

**Catching defenders cold:** Springing an early surprise move when defenders are still feeling their way into the game.

**Defending deep:** When a team elects to concede ground to the opposition once possession has been lost, and adopts a defensive line deep in its own half.

**Defensive line:** The imaginary line linking the defenders together.

**Forced inside:** A wide attacker in possession is forced to carry or play the ball into the central area due to the defender positioning himself in such a way as to inhibit further progress up the wing.

**Holding the defensive line:** In trying to maintain close proximity between the defense and the midfield, the defense will occasionally hold their ground allowing opposing forwards to run into offside positions.

**Inside shoulder marking position:** Where a defender positions himself between the attacker and the goal being defended, thus looking over the inside shoulder of the attacker i.e. the shoulder nearest the center line of the field.

**Man in the hole:** A player occupying a position just behind the central striker(s).

**Man-to-man marking:** A defensive system where defenders are allocated a particular opponent to cover or mark throughout a game.

**Outside channels:** The area between the forward and the nearest sideline. In this context, defenders are prone to take the 'inside' marking position/line i.e. positioning themselves between the forward and the goal.

**Outside shoulder marking position:** Where a defender positions himself looking over the shoulder of the attacker nearest the sideline, thus inhibiting passes into wider wing areas.

**Play off:** Feeding from, and playing a complimentary role to, a teammate.

**Pulling/peeling off the shoulder:** When a forward tries to position himself beyond or behind a defender who is trying simultaneously to watch the ball.

**Showing the inside:** Involves channeling the opponent in possession into central areas in front of the defense, where limited space exists to develop penetrating attacks.

**Showing the outside:** Involves channeling opponents in possession into wide wing areas and away from the goal being defended.

**Stepping up:** Refers to the last defender, or the defensive line as a whole, stepping up in front of a forward to catch him offside.

**Tracking:** Following or covering an opponent.

**Zonal marking:** When players are allocated areas, as opposed to particular opponents, to patrol.

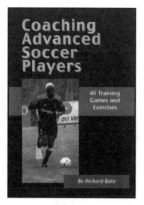
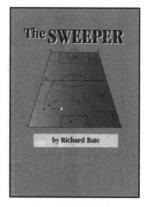

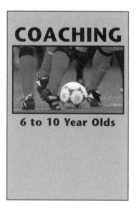
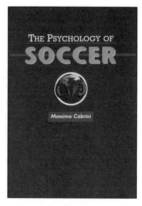
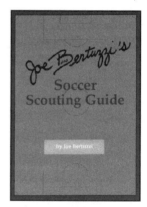

# NEW Coaching Books from REEDSWAIN

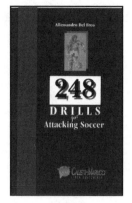

**#261**
**Match Analysis**
**and Game Preparation**
*Henny Kormelink*
*and Tjeu Seevrens*
**$12.95**

**#291**
**Soccer Fitness Training**
*by Enrico Arcelli*
*and Ferretto Ferretti*
**$12.95**

**#794**
**248 Drills for**
**Attacking Soccer**
*by Alessandro Del Freo*
**$14.95**

# Bestselling Coaching Books

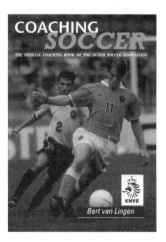

**#185**
**Conditioning**
**for Soccer**
*Dr. Raymond Verheijen*
**$19.95**

**#154:**
**Coaching Soccer**
*by Bert van Lingen*
**$14.95**

**#177:**
PRINCIPLES OF
**Brazilian Soccer**
*by José Thadeu Goncalves*
*in cooperation with Prof. Julio Mazzei*
**$16.95**

# Bestselling Coaching Books

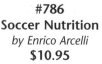